The Subconscious, The Divine,
and
Me

A spiritual guide for the
day-to-day pilgrim

Joseph D. Drumheller

Pine Winds Press

An imprint of Idyll Arbor, Inc.
39129 264th Ave SE, Enumclaw, WA 98022
www.PineWindsPress.com

Idyll Arbor Editor: Thomas M. Blaschko
Cover photo: Peter Bowers

ISBN: 9780937663240

Printed in the United States of America

Library of Congress Cataloging-in-Publication Data

Drumheller, Joseph D., 1959-
    The subconscious, the divine, and me : a spiritual guide for the day-to-day pilgrim / Joseph D. Drumheller.
        p. cm.
    Includes bibliographical references.
    ISBN 978-0-937663-24-0 (alk. paper)
    1. Mental healing. 2. Spiritual healing. 3. Mind and body. I. Title.
RZ400.D78 2011
615.8'528--dc23

2011051485

To Tamara

For teaching me

The meaning of belief

Contents

Acknowledgments

First and foremost, my thanks go to *Tamara Zink*. Without her love and support I'd be nowhere. In deep gratitude, I also want to acknowledge my Corbin/Drumheller ancestry and my immediate families for setting the foundation for growth, stretching me beyond what I thought possible, teaching me where I need to develop, helping me understand forgiveness, and learning what love is and is not (I'm still working that one out).

I'm deeply indebted to each client I've had the opportunity to work with. They are my teachers. Much of what I have learned has come through them. I also acknowledge, with deep thanks, Oneness University for popping the cork to deeper levels of spirituality that changed my life forever.

More thanks to:

Ananda Giri and Tony Robbins — for personal miracles that defy description

Bev Edie — for artwork, T, being my friend and one of my deepest revered teachers

Carol Brumet and the PeaceHealth Cancer Center in Bellingham, WA — for the opportunity to work on a very deep level

Chris Morgan — for playing his part in one of the coolest synchronistic connections that helped get this book published

Courtney Seard, Abby Soley, Mark Butterworth — for teaching me how to be a healer

Flora LaRayne – for her gentle healing, insight and guidance

Fran Bolt — who helped start this ball rolling

Jacklyn Johnston — for powerful help in my own healing and development work

Natasha Haycock-Chavez — not sure why, but hey, it's my book and I can thank anyone I like!

Tom Blaschko and *Idyll Arbor Inc.* — for making me a published author

Oh yes, and *The Divine* — for making it all work

Introduction

I decided to write this book for four reasons.

First, every winter for the past six years, I've built a boat — nice cedar strip canoes, works of art actually. Recently, I moved into a place without a workspace and nowhere to build a boat. I've also developed a gnarly allergic reaction to epoxy. To put it simply, I can't build boats anymore, so I have extra time on my hands.

Second, I have a secret. I think I've figured out the nuts and bolts to living practical spirituality, how to do it on a day-to-day basis in a regular life…without incense! I've kept this secret so long that it's starting to bug me. In fact, the Divine has been encouraging me lately to get the word out. I've got all this extra time on my hands and no place to build a boat. I can take a hint: It's time to write!

The third and most important reason is to help you (the reader) discover and develop your own connection to Divine presence, an absolutely necessary skill to lead a happy, healthy, purposeful life. In a broader perspective, in order for humanity to emerge from this time of transition, this Divine connection must be the cornerstone experience.

And my last reason for writing this book? Because Tamara told me to!

This book has no affiliation with any given religion, though I frequently refer to a benevolent presence that's bigger than all of us. There are a million historical words for it: the Divine, Chi, the Great Spirit, Collective Consciousness, Higher Self, Source, God…you name it. I've never found a word that completely sits right with me. So to make it simple, I'll use "Divine." *I name my God.*

I've laid this book out as a series of cookbook-style "lessons" because my peanut-sized brain likes to make sense of things by connecting the dots. However, we all know life isn't so neatly cut and dried. More often than not, you'll discover in the living of life that these carefully devised "lessons" don't follow any particular order. They frequently overlap and weave in and out of one another.

I've used a few stories in places to help the text flow and to keep the material from becoming too heavy, dry, or boring. With the exception of the Pre-Lesson and Lesson #5, none of the stories you read here are real. Rather, they are a mishmash of hypothetical situations that I have comprised from my own personal experience or bits and pieces I've accumulated through hundreds and hundreds of sessions. Healing is based on trust, and I protect client confidentially absolutely.

In the pages ahead, I'll be sharing knowledge and experience from over two decades of working with the human subconscious — work that has consistently produced positive results in the physical world of healing. Some of the information presented here, about 10 percent of it, has been acquired through reading and attending courses. The remainder of my knowledge has been gained from personal experience. I've lived through these lessons. I've suffered deeply, as we all have. I've learned, I've healed, and I've grown. Call it luck or fate, but I've had the incredible opportunity to be on both sides of the inner journey fence as a student, client, facilitator, and teacher. Growth stops for no one; there is no going backwards. Awareness and experience, driven by Divine grace, are the keys. We are here to grow into happiness. So, shall we begin?

God's-grace

Pre-Lesson
Keep Your Eyes on the Prize

Let's Eat Dessert First!

"Why bother with spirituality? It seems like a pretty strange and ambiguous venture. I've never really understood it anyway. I mean, what's the point?"

Let me answer with a story.

Last summer, I went to check my e-mail at the local library. It's only about a half-block from my office, and I go there all the time. On the way over, I bumped into a client I had assisted through his cancer treatment. The work we had done together went exceptionally well, and his recovery into full remission was amazing. After doing subconscious healing work with him for a couple of months, he decided to quit chemotherapy completely. He later had a successful reverse colostomy bag surgery, which is very rare. And now he's doing fine.

While we were chirping away on the sidewalk, another former client of mine walked by and joined in the conversation. I hadn't seen him for seven years. He was another cancer recovery patient...full remission.

As we spoke, we realized what we had all been through together. Life and death — or rather, death and life.

Everyone was beaming. I was beaming to see them both alive and to have had a hand in their recovery; they were beaming because they had survived. It was a moment of experienced collective joy, one I'll never forget.

Joy, happiness, excitement, passion, purpose, meaning, peace, contentment, fulfillment, abundance, freedom, etc., etc., etc. How many of us get to experience these words, let alone live them out on a daily basis? Not nearly enough. The adventure we're about to embark on will lead into the realm of these words. It's the sole reason for taking up a spiritual path: to increase the quality of life. Try to keep that in mind.

Spiritual and personal growth takes time. It takes focus, commitment, and even some skill. I'm not going to pull any punches; it can be difficult, especially in the beginning. However, that's why I'm here. I'm here to guide you through the process and help you avoid bumps along the way. The effort you put in will produce noticeable results in your daily life. It will also influence the lives of everyone you come in contact with. So if you're interested in making your life and the world a better place, then by all means, please join me.

Pre-Lesson Homework

You thought you were going to get out of homework? No way! So, snuggle up in a cozy chair with your favorite pen, a cup of hot cocoa, a fuzzy blanket, and we'll begin.

Take a few moments and answer this question: "At this point in my life, what does spirituality mean to me?" Hint: This is a trick question. Save you answer.

Lesson #1
Pain Leads to Suffering

Watch Out for the Dog Poo!

Okay, so how many of you out there have never felt pain? Go ahead, raise your hands. Hmm…just what I thought, nobody. Unless you were born enlightened, the road to eternal joy, peace, and happiness begins with pain. This is a seemingly unfortunate part of the human condition. However, the good news is that most pain is only in your head. That is to say, the ache of life starts in the human mind. Allow me to explain the best I can.

I don't pretend to be an expert on the intimate and mysterious workings of the human mind. What I propose to do is lay out a simple theory that has proven to be a very effective model. Keep in mind that theories are just theories and are subject to modification at any time. This one has worked well for me over the last couple of decades.

The Conscious Mind — Noise, Noise, Noise!

Each and every one of us on planet Earth walks around in this little bubble called the human mind. On the outer layer of the bubble is the conscious mind, a very important and influential part of our existence that differentiates us from animals. It's our "awake" state of mind, the state where we spend the majority of our waking hours. It's the home of our cognitive and rational thinking process and our ability to organize and categorize. Much of our society is steeped in the conscious mind, including science and modern medicine.

The following list is borrowed from Yvonne Oswald's book, *Every Word Has Power*, detailing features of the conscious mind. The conscious mind:

1. Is aware of what it perceives.
2. Contacts reality through the five senses.
3. Gathers and sorts information.
4. Communicates to the Divine through the subconscious.
5. Thinks deductively.
6. Makes choices and judgments.
7. Reviews information and draws conclusions.
8. Makes generalizations.
9. Likes to analyze and categorize.
10. Requests information from the subconscious.

The conscious mind is an incredible thinking machine. It just doesn't stop. My favorite description of the mind's activity is written by Eckhart Tolle in *A New Earth:* "Thinking isn't something you do; thinking is something that happens to you." Many of these thoughts are unfocused noise and chatter. Mind chatter can range from mildly annoying to downright debilitating. There are numerous self-help books out there that encourage us to train ourselves to think positively. However, due to the sheer volume of thought we have, our control over mental chatter is fairly limited. Simply recognizing mental chatter and the effect it has on your life is the first step in learning to dissipate its power. If the chatter is excessively noisy, there is likely a strong underlying emotional charge.

About six months ago, I moved into a new apartment. Before moving in, I let the landlord know I had a couple of canoes that required storage. "No problem," he said, "just throw them behind the shed." When I checked it out, I noticed there were already a couple of old kayaks back there. They were in pretty sad shape. Both were partially hidden by weeds, and exposure to the elements had taken its toll. Clearly, they hadn't been used for some time.

Without asking, I cleared the weeds and moved his kayaks to the more visible side of the shed. I seized the prime storage space and put my canoes in the more secure and choice spot, where the kayaks had been stored.

A couple days later, I went to load up a canoe and noticed that one of the kayaks was missing. After I moved it to the more visible side of the shed, somebody saw it and ripped it off. I felt incredibly guilty, realizing I shouldn't have moved those kayaks in the first place. I even went to the trouble of moving the remaining kayak back to where it was.

My mind started going crazy: *Should I tell the landlord? He never used them anyway. He didn't even bother to lock them up. But it kind of was my fault for moving them. Is he going to want me to pay for it?* I decided to do nothing, but the ramblings in my head grew stronger and crazier for about a week.

While all this madness was going on inside my head, I realized I had a very strong emotional charge coming up. I felt like I was in trouble for something I had done wrong, felt it right in my chest. This was big. This scenario had been repeating throughout my entire life with spouses, employers, teachers, and coaches. It obviously started with my dad and was subconsciously projected onto every authority figure I ever encountered — even my landlord!

As soon as that realization occurred, I knew what to do. I had to release the charge (we'll get into the mechanics of that a little later), and when I did, I felt relieved. Only then did an opportunity for healing occur.

After that, I changed my mind and decided to tell my landlord. About that time, I saw him behind the shed and figured it would be an opportune moment to spill the beans. When I approached, I saw he was returning the old kayak. He had taken it for his niece and nephew who were visiting that week.

Remember the old cartoons where the character turns into a sucker after he's been duped? That was exactly how I felt, except I had been duped by my own mind — a mind that shook me like a rag doll for a week. *Sucker! Ha-ha!* Not only was the kayak never stolen, but nobody knew or cared. It was all in my head, amplified by an enormous emotional charge. I was the star in my own drama, and I could have won an academy award.

There has been a lot of work probing into the wild world of calming conscious mind noise, which is well beyond the scope of this book. However, I'd like to mention two sources that have crossed my path: Oneness University and "The Work," developed by Byron Katie. These two resources, listed in the reference section of this book, are well worth checking out.

The Subconscious Mind

Underlying the conscious mind in the human mind bubble is the subconscious mind. By definition, we are not normally aware of this aspect of our being (*sub* means *under*). While we are busy going about our day, deeply engrossed in the conscious mind, the subconscious mind lies quietly beneath the surface. It's the home of the **nonphysical** realms of the human experience. Some aspects include our dreams, emotions, ideas, and imagination.

The following list is borrowed from Yvonne Oswald's book, *Every Word Has Power*, detailing features of the subconscious. The subconscious mind:

1. Operates the physical body.
2. Has a direct connection with the Divine.
3. Remembers everything.
4. Stores emotions in the physical body.
5. Maintains genealogical instincts.
6. Creates and maintains least effort (repeating patterns).
7. Uses metaphor, imagery, and symbols.
8. Takes direction from the conscious mind.

9. Accepts information literally and personally.
10. Does not process negative commands.

In addition to those features listed above, the subconscious mind also holds our **perceptions**, subconscious beliefs of *who we think we are as people and how we think the world operates*. In other words, whoever we think we are as people and however we think the world operates quietly lives under the conscious mind in the subconscious. Our perceptions may be wonderful or painful. The subconscious mind does not evaluate or judge these perceptions; it simply accepts them as truth. Furthermore, the job of the subconscious mind is to play these perceptions out in the circumstances of our lives. Creating our perceptions is what the subconscious is designed to do. Whoever you think you are as person and however you think the world operates will be reflected back to you in the events of your life.

Whoa…wait a minute! The first time I heard that, two things went off in my head: one good and one not so good. First off, it made sense. Second, it explained why my life resembled a train wreck. I felt doomed from the get-go, helpless to do anything about it. If you feel the same way, hang on a minute. Don't panic…yet. Keep reading. It gets better.

The Critical Faculty of the Mind

Because the subconscious mind is such a continuously creative machine and the conscious mind is limited in its scope, this puts us all in a very vulnerable situation. If every subconscious perception we experienced were to be acted out in our daily lives, we would be living nothing but the

Chaos Theory in motion! Just like traffic in India! Therefore, somewhere in the wisdom of creating the human experience, the critical faculty of the mind was established to prevent us all from going absolutely nuts.

The critical faculty of the mind is an invisible, protective barrier living somewhere between the conscious and subconscious minds. Its function is to constantly evaluate perceptions that are projected in our direction: in thought, word, or action. As perceptions are aimed our way, the critical faculty will judge it as yes or no. Yes means the projection is in harmony with what lives in the subconscious mind. No means the projected perception is not in harmony with what's in our subconscious. When a yes perception arrives, the critical faculty will open up and allow the perception in, thereby allowing the existing perception to grow. When a no perception shows up, the critical faculty will remain up, rejecting the perception as an untruth.

Let me give you an example: If I teach a workshop and someone comes up to me and says, "Wow that was great. You're a wonderful teacher," my critical faculty will let down and permit that perception to enter. My subconscious perception of *I'm a wonderful teacher* (i.e. *I'm a wonderful person*) will grow and continue to manifest in the events of my life. However, if someone in my class is sitting in the back row thinking, *Boy, this guy's an idiot*, my critical faculty will remain up and reject that projection as an untruth. It simply does not fit my perception of myself or how I view the world.

The incredibly strange part of the critical faculty is that it appears to be fully established by the time we're about four years old. **What?!?** The first time I read that, I almost broke down and cried. What a gyp! You mean, by the time we're only out of our toddler years, whoever we think we are as people and however we think the world operates is nearly set in stone? And the shaping of us poor little human beings is totally at the mercy of our immediate families and environment? Afraid so. It's a case of karma. For some reason, who knows why, our immediate environment is *the* integral foundation of our human experience. It's where our learning begins.

Negative Perceptions — Subconscious Emotional Charges

I have seen negative or painful perceptions referred to as "charged emotions" and the "pain body" by Oneness University and Eckhart Tolle, respectively. I prefer the Oneness term because it most accurately fits the healing work I have done. So from here on out, I'll refer to painful subconscious perceptions as **charged emotions** or **emotional charges**.

Let's take a look at Suzie. She's a two-year-old girl, and today is a major red-letter day in her life. She gets to drink milk out of a real glass — not one of those little-kid plastic sippy cups, but a real glass container. Suzie's mom is at the stove cooking dinner. She's had a hectic day, working a job that barely enables her to make ends meet. She's been a single mom for the past eighteen months and hasn't seen a dime of child support for Suzie or her two siblings. Needless to say, mom's life is on stress overload. As she cooks dinner, low and behold, Suzie drops her glass. Milk and shattered glass go everywhere. Mom, at her wit's end, spins toward Suzie and screams, "Damn it! You'll never amount to anything!!!" *Blink.* A negative perception, or charged emotion, has just been created in Suzie's subconscious mind. The critical faculty has also built a wall around that perception to protect it. Does that mean Suzie will grow up to be worthless? Of course not! However, if she continues to receive the same message over and over again as she grows up (in thought, word, or action), the critical faculty will continue to let down, allowing that charged emotion to grow — to the point where it will eventually begin to appear in the events of her daily life. Perhaps she won't be able to hold down a job; she may go from one failed relationship to the next; or it may show up as a physical illness or injury. The subconscious mind can be very creative when it comes to expressing emotional charges, and it doesn't stop...until the charges are gone.

So you may be thinking, *What, exactly, is an emotional charge?* **Subconscious emotional charges are un-experienced, subconsciously repressed feelings that produce pain.** Examples include hurt, rage, anxiety, rejection, shame, unworthiness, fear, depression, and abandonment, and the list goes on and on. These are like living entities in our bodies, and they won't go away until they are experienced fully.

Human Suffering

Let's take subconscious emotional charges one step further and journey into the world of suffering. First, it's essential to understand what suffering actually is. Is freedom from suffering the end of pain, anger, and unpleasant emotion, replaced by everlasting bliss? Sorry, but no. That wouldn't be very realistic or very human. Suffering is not pain, but the avoidance of it. Let me say that again: The definition of suffering is the avoidance of pain. Pain demands attention, and when it is avoided, it repeats itself over and over again. Suffering is the experience of the same repeating pain. Herein resides the grand paradox. In order to overcome suffering, you must experience your pain fully.

Human beings are designed for growth and experiencing life to the fullest. That includes *all* of our emotions. Pain, jealousy, anger, enthusiasm, joy, contentment, etc., are all part of the human experience. Look at small child who drops his/her ice cream cone on the sidewall. A few moments of intense agony are guaranteed. However, in just a few minutes, after the emotion has been experienced, the tears dry, and the child is back to experiencing life in the moment. When emotions are experienced fully, they dissipate. The problem arises when we avoid experiencing unpleasant emotions. We essentially put them in the closet to reemerge at a later date…and they do.

How many of us know someone who has gone from relationship to relationship, experiencing the same problems? How about the person who avoids conflict with authority to the point of becoming seriously ill? They are just avoiding unpleasant feelings. We've all done it. In fact, it's a natural response. Unpleasant emotions tend to get repressed into the subconscious without conscious knowledge or intention on our part. When that happens, they get stuck in the subconscious. The subconscious then continues to re-create uncomfortable circumstances in our lives so that the repressed emotions can be experienced. Without awareness, this saga can last a lifetime.

Repeating Patterns — Props in Your One-Person Drama

I'm a fairly sensitive guy. I have emotions running through me all the time. When I first became aware of my internal process, my big question was: How do I know if I have an emotional charge or just a random feeling? The answer is simple: repeating patterns. If you have difficult emotions repeating themselves in similar circumstances, regardless of the people you are dealing with, it's a subconscious emotional charge. Examples may include a woman from an abusive family who keeps finding an abusive partner or a man with an impoverished father that can't ever seem to get his act together with finances.

The combinations and possibilities are endless. There's a potential charge for every difficult life circumstance. It takes a certain commitment to honest self-reflection to discover that your repeating patterns are actually your own subconscious invention! Emotional charges are *never* about the other person. They are your creation and experience only. Other people who trigger your emotional charges are only props in your own one-person drama.

Tragic Events

Let's dive straight into an atheistic argument, a question that can rack the faith of even the most devout believer. What about suffering caused by birth defects, starvation, tsunamis, landslides, earthquakes, and disease? How does this nifty little subconscious mind and suffering theory explain random cataclysmic events of tragedy?

The truth is, it doesn't. Remember, for some reason, pain is part of the human experience. However, learning to experience pain prevents it from recurring over and over again. Sometimes it's not easy, but as we will discover, it's the road to the Divine.

Lesson #1 — Homework

Take a few moments to sit and contemplate. You can journal, if that's your style. Think of the most significant difficulties you've had in your life or troubles you may be experiencing now. If you hit a snag, you needn't look far. Most of us don't need to search any farther than our own immediate families.

Can you see any repeating patterns? Are you aware of any emotion that has been repressed?

That's all for Lesson #1 homework. And believe me...that's plenty for now.

Lesson #2
Suffering Leads to Awareness

Ooh, I Think I'm getting it!

Most of us are not aware of subconscious charges, let alone how they drive our decision-making and behavior. However, once we begin to understand our tendency to avoid pain and embrace suffering, what's next? Now we look inside ourselves to recognize our subconscious emotional charges, where they come from, and how they affect our conduct, psyche, and bodies. *Becoming aware of emotional charges is the first step to end human suffering!*

Where Does Suffering Come From?

The Source of Suffering Is Separation

The ultimate root of suffering lies in separation from the Divine. Somewhere in the evolution of the human species, the natural connection to the Divine (and to who we genuinely are) got lost. Perhaps it began with the overdevelopment of the conscious mind and the creation of mind chatter. Maybe it was the result of our inclination to separate ourselves from Nature. Whatever the cause, the entire purpose of subconscious healing is to reestablish that connection. It's the road home.

Suffering Is in the Past

When we begin to grasp the notion that suffering is repeating patterns caused by subconsciously repressed pain, the light bulb should go on that says, "Hey, wait a minute…*if* suffering is just repeating patterns, then it's really based in the past." Ding-ding! We have a winner.

In a way, suffering isn't actually real. The past doesn't exist. Suffering is from the past. You do the math. How much of our behavior and decision-making is based on something that technically isn't real? A lot! Every time someone reacts to a recurring difficult situation, it's just a response to the past. It's like fighting ghosts; there's nothing there but a mental image and a feeling. The problem is that those images and feelings can be *extremely* strong.

Here's a fairly typical scenario I've seen a number of young adults go through. In fact, I was guilty of it myself throughout my twenties. For entertainment's sake, let's call this young buck Hugo. He was a recent transplant from Florida to my little town in the Pacific Northwest. I met Hugo through my circle of paddling pals, so we went out a few times and hit the river together. Getting to know him, I discovered he came from an extremely abusive past. He hated his old man and, as far as I could figure, with good reason. That was why Hugo picked up and moved to the Northwest, "to get as far away from that son-of-a-!!!!! as possible."

I also heard Hugo talking about his employer. If I hadn't known the context of the conversation, I would have sworn he was talking about his father. It wasn't too long until he moved to another town about 150 miles away, stating something to the effect of "My boss is a jerk" and "I'm outta here." A few months later, he moved to Alaska. Last I heard, Hugo was in Australia, still fighting the same issues with authority figures (i.e. his father).

This is a case of repeating patterns caused by a subconscious emotional charge created in the past. The most effective way for Hugo to break his repeating pattern of misery is to go into the subconscious mind and heal his emotional world.

Childhood — It's Not Your Fault

Most emotional charges are planted in us by someone else or some outside event. When? When we're most vulnerable, of course. Emotional vulnerability is at its peak before the critical faculty of the mind is developed. As you may recall, that takes place in very early childhood, when the subconscious mind is completely exposed.

We enter this world as pure vessels, wide open and absorbing life like a sponge. This includes the good, the bad, and the ugly. Hey, nobody said life was fair. The stork settles a few of our darlings into lovely, cushy feather beds. Others get dumped into this world under absolutely horrendous circumstances. Wherever we land is where our journey begins, like it or not, and our emotional charges develop at the whim of our surroundings.

It's not a difficult stretch to come to the conclusion that I can't emphasize strongly enough: Your suffering is not your fault. You did not create your problems, dysfunction, or disease. You are only responding to circumstances at your given level of awareness.

Let's take it one step further. In regard to the person(s) who planted charges in you, it's not their fault either. They were also responding to their charges at their given level of awareness. Take it as far back as you need to go. Who is ultimately responsible? Nobody. Suffering isn't anybody's fault; it just is. You may not believe it now, but suffering is actually what paves the road to the Divine.

Ancestry — It's Truly Not Your Fault

We inherit all sorts of stuff from out family: appearance, size, shape, character, behavior, mentality, and if we're lucky, a little money. We never asked for any of it. It's just what's on the menu. We also inherit from our ancestry through the subconscious, including emotional charges.

We all know someone who's a spitting image of their parents, a regular clone, or a chip off the ol' block. I knew a girl in high school whose mother's maiden name was Smith. She later married a guy named Smythe, who ironically (or maybe not so ironically) resembled her dad. Her mother had three kids, all girls. She had three kids, all boys. Listing the similarities between those two would take all day. If you take a look within your own family or your friends' families, recognizing generational parallels will begin to be surreal.

For some, inherited ancestral traits can skip a generation. I have an acquaintance whose grandfather was a bit of a bigwig powerbroker, married three times. My acquaintance never met him and resented growing up in his shadow. Oddly enough, he's at the beginning of his third marriage, and his life is moving onto a significant public platform. His level of influence was born into him. He's had to do quite a bit of soul-searching and forgiveness to accept himself as a part of his heritage. The more he has accepted himself and his pedigree, the more his destiny of success has unfolded.

"So what's the point? We inherit traits from our families. Everybody knows that." Not only do we inherit physical and behavioral characteristics, but we also subconsciously inherit emotion. And what does that mean? It means we also inherit suffering. Some of our suffering is caused by an unusual subconscious connection to our heritage. Understanding this possibility opens the potential for subconscious healing to a whole new level. So far, we've learned that suffering is basically not our fault. Furthermore, if we inherit suffering from ancestors who were dead and buried long ago, then it's *really* not our fault.

Gestation

"I've always been close to my mom, but I never knew how close." Before birth we *are* our mother. We're connected physically, physiologically, emotionally, and subconsciously. It's not uncommon to absorb our mother's emotional charges while we're in the womb, especially if the contributing events are traumatic.

Here's a hypothetical scenario I've seen repeated is a variety of situations. Since most of us have had spouses and lovers at least once or twice in our lives, I'll use the context of an intimate relationship, something we can all relate to.

A young woman came to see me for recurring anxiety attacks that were happening at an accelerated and stronger rate. They exploded into her life whenever she crossed some ambiguous line of going from a romantic to a committed relationship. It had ruined several previous relationships. She was now involved with a man she genuinely loved. The attacks were becoming so frequent and so strong that she could barely function. She was desperate.

This was in the early days of my practice, back when I took more of an analytical approach to subconscious healing. Over the course of a few sessions, we probed into the events of her childhood and had some initial satisfactory success. However, the anxiety attacks still came back, albeit with less frequency and intensity. I couldn't put my finger on what was behind this. We just didn't seem to be getting to the core of the problem.

In conversation, I asked about her parents, and that led to the topic of their divorce. The split happened rather abruptly, and it was rather grueling on her mother. I asked her how old she was when her parents broke up, to which she replied, "Oh, I wasn't born yet. I was still in my mom's tummy." Flash! Maybe she picked up emotional charges from her mom while she was pregnant. By the next session, her anxiety attacks gone...permanently.

Family, Societal, and Media Conditioning

"All of us Kennedys are politicians…To get a good job, you need a good education…My TV would never lie to me." Family, societal, and media conditioning is lathered upon us from the moment we enter this world.

What is conditioning? It's received input through word, thought, or action that influences our behavior. When we receive a message over and over again (especially when we're very young), it enters the subconscious and will eventually be acted out in our lives. It's not necessarily good or bad. Problems arise when the input received from our surroundings (family, society, media) doesn't fit who we are as people. This creates internal conflict and puts us at odds with ourselves and our world, which is — you guessed it — a subconscious emotional charge.

Family
"We've been lawyers in this family as long as I can remember. My dad, his dad, his dad's dad. We go back generations. By God, you'll be one too!" That may be fine for my brother Seymour, but I'm just not wired that way. I need to beat to my own free-spirited drum. For me, becoming a lawyer would be a straight shot to hell.

Families can be blown apart by adherence to family conditioning, especially if it supersedes genuine needs. How many of us know someone who has gone into the family business and hated every minute of it? How many of us have been crushed by family disapproval over something we were genuinely passionate about? If we are to grow and mature into the people we are meant to be in this life, we need to listen to the voice within. It may or may not be in accordance with family approval. Blind adherence to family conditioning, at the expense of yourself, can produce a lifetime of suffering.

Society

"Man is mad." That's one of my favorite quotes I picked up at Oneness University. Because each of us projects the circumstances of emotional charges into our lives, many societal values are tainted with the spewing of these charges. It can be a vicious cycle that propagates even more suffering. Collective values get filtered through the charges and chattering minds of millions. Ideals behind a societal system can easily be polluted into the perpetuation of things like needless war and excessive corporate greed. It's no wonder the state of affairs can get so messy. As each of us goes, so goes society. In order to transform our world, we must transform ourselves on the inside. As we do, our values will shift. Emphasis will then be placed more on the quality of life and less on the trappings of the conscious mind and unresolved emotion.

Media

Pop Quiz! Answer the following:

Twenty-second-century historians refer to the early twenty-first century as:

A) The age of ultimate distraction.

B) The period when humanity finally separated itself completely from its natural physical environment.

C) When the conscious mind went absolutely ballistic.

D) All of the above.

(Answer: D)

Technology? Yikes! Talk about a runaway freight train. Don't get me wrong, I love it — or at least parts of it. I can't denounce technology as I sit here pecking away on my laptop. Let's admit it: we're hooked. What's worse is that our kids are hooked. Most kids nowadays are more familiar with some flat, illuminated screen than members of their own extended families. If I were to ask my sixteen-year-old stepdaughter today, "What was the weather like this morning?" or "What phase is the moon in right now?" she would probably answer, "Uhh...I don't know, but I have thirty new friends on Facebook!"

We are absolutely hammered every day with electronic media. The media tells us what to do, how to be, who to be with, where to spend our money, and that violence is acceptable. And, boy, is it effective. When we watch TV, surf the web, or play on our phones, we go into a mild trance state. When we're in a trance, our subconscious is open. This allows images, sounds, and emotions to come right in and attach themselves to the framework of our belief system. It's extremely difficult not to be subconsciously influenced by media. It is creating and shaping our era. Let's face it: We wouldn't have cell phones without *Star Trek*. Again, this is neither good nor bad. The question is, "Does this influence produce suffering in our personal world?" This question falls back on the awareness of subconscious emotional charges.

Past Lives

A couple years ago, I visited India, a country steeped in the belief of reincarnation. That pervasive belief permeates their entire society, but it's a bit of a two-edged sword. In many instances, a person from India wouldn't bat an eye over things Westerners get completely stressed about. On the other hand, there's not a lot of motivation to get things done. You can always do it in your next life!

I'm not sure about where I stand on reincarnation, but as a healer, it doesn't really matter. Can suffering originate in a past life? Maybe. However, entertaining the notion in subconscious healing provides some enormous benefits. It allows clients to step completely outside of the context and mental framework of their present-day lives and gain an entirely new perspective on their own suffering. It's a way to detach in order to let go.

Let's imagine a young man came to me for a chronic condition that stumped medical doctors. There was no logical explanation for the incredible pain he felt in his body. When he finally arrived at my door, he had been through numerous examinations and a treasure chest full of medications.

Between his work with me and another local alternative healthcare professional, he was able to heal about 90 percent of the pain over the course of a year. His biggest breakthrough came during a past-life regression session. It was huge. The experience gave him the opportunity to completely reframe the context of his life. It was absolute freedom. Somehow, in the context of that liberty, he was able to free an enormous amount of physical pain. The connection between his stored subconscious emotion and physical pain was released.

Trauma

As previously mentioned, emotional charges can enter the subconscious before the critical faculty of the mind is formed in early childhood. Charges can also enter when the critical faculty is let down. This can occur in times of shock and excessive trauma. Examples may include sudden physical injury, surgery, or receiving unexpected shocking news. When we're stunned, we enter a trance. The critical faculty relaxes, allowing negative emotional information into the subconscious. In my experience and for reasons I don't completely understand, traumatic events are not uncommon around the ages of two, fourteen, and twenty.

The Unknown

Sometimes, understanding the cause of an emotional charge can accelerate subconscious healing. However, every now and then, you can psychologize, analyze, and snoop around for sources of pain without ever finding the source. Luckily, in terms of alleviating subconscious pain, finding the cause isn't absolutely necessary. As we'll learn in Lesson #3, simply locating the feeling of emotional pain in the body is enough.

Noteworthy Subconscious Emotional Charge Issues

Before we dive into the process of freeing yourself from subconscious emotional charges and the suffering that accompanies them, let's take a peek at a few charges that many of us experience. The list below includes issues I've had significant firsthand experience in helping people overcome.

Abandonment

Because we're born absolutely dependent, the fear of being left alone is almost instinctual. We're not designed to be isolated. We can't survive by ourselves. In a way, being alone isn't really human.

Ironically, we come into this life alone, and we go out alone. We must also face every life transition by ourselves. Sooner or later, everyone gets kicked out of the nest. To fully mature, we have to stand on our own two feet, and it's not always easy.

In regard to abandonment, subconscious emotional charges can be created when there isn't a loving presence to guide us through early phases of childhood. We're too vulnerable, innocent, and ill-equipped to understand or handle initial life transitions on our own. When we're forced to do so, the resulting subconscious fear can cause debilitating circumstances in our adult lives.

Imagine a young man whose father was not around when he was born. In fact, he wasn't around much at all. As a boy, he was frequently told, "Go play outside," and he wasn't allowed to come back inside until suppertime. The time of year or weather conditions didn't matter. He was left unsupervised and alone all day. Fortunately, he lived near some woods, so he wasn't turned directly out onto the streets. Instinctively, he secured hiding places for food and money, in case he wasn't allowed to return back home for good someday, and he grew up tough and afraid.

Two things happened when he matured into an adult. First, he developed incredible independence and resolve. He could take care of himself in any situation. Second, he couldn't bear to be on his own for any extended period of time. The subconscious emotional charges he carried from his youth produced absolute terror when he was left alone. He eventually became very successful in a business that required extensive travel. However, he had multiple lovers stashed in different cities, just like the food and money he used to hide in the woods. He was never alone.

Unworthiness, Rejection, and Insecurity — Lack of Love

This one is a biggie because most of us get at least one helping of it. None of us get enough love. It's just not possible. We enter this world completely dependent on someone else, physically and emotionally, twenty-four hours a day, seven days a week. There hasn't been one set of parents in all of human history who has had the ability to satisfy the insatiable needs of an infant. It truly does take a village to raise a child. Add another kid or two into the mix and forget about it.

We grow up competing for love and attention. We'll do anything to get it. We'll be perfect, troublesome, depressed, sick, hurt, or even a superstar. Throwing some parental neglect and abuse on this ravenous need can produce some deeply seated emotional charges.

Unworthiness can be expressed in a variety of ways but tends to gravitate into two extremes: under- and overachieving. This is not only limited to jobs and careers; it can also spill into relationships. Examples may include the workaholic executive who is always vying for supervisor approval or someone who continues to sabotage seemingly healthy intimate relationships. The underlying message is the same: I'm not worthy.

The Broken Heart — Grieving

Life is a never-ending parade of hanging on and letting go, letting go and hanging on. In fact, to be happy, healthy, and well adjusted, we need to learn the art of letting go. It's imperative to learn how to grieve.

At some point in life, we discover that being human means being brokenhearted. We love and become emotionally attached. When we lose someone or something we love, it can be very painful, resulting in deep grief. It can be over anything: a person, an object, our innocence, a pet, a part of ourselves, circumstances, etc. It arrives in waves over a period of time. Just when you think you're finished, along comes another wave. It can take weeks, months, or even years. The timeframe is different for everyone.

A variety of emotions are experienced during the grieving process. They may include shock, denial, sadness, loneliness, depression, anger, and at some point hopefully, acceptance, a decision to move on, forgiveness, and peace. Problems arise when we don't allow ourselves to grieve. This can be due to lack of awareness or flat-out refusal to experience difficult emotions. In either case, the suppression of emotion will create an emotional charge in the subconscious. The charge will then continue to repeat itself over time, until it's experienced.

There are times when life can be difficult. Grieving is one of them. In the framework of spiritual growth, grieving is not a time to shy away from the work that needs to done. It's a time to allow yourself, as gently as possible, to feel the feelings of loss and let them go. It's an act of honoring yourself and what you have lost.

Physical Illness — Cancer

Subconscious emotional charges can be felt in the body. Perhaps you feel stress in your stomach, rage in your head, or sadness in your heart. The charges need an outlet, a way to be experienced and released. When suppressed, they can find that outlet through the body in the form of illness, instead of just through life circumstance.

I've worked extensively with cancer patients over the past decade, and both of my parents died from the disease. When someone is diagnosed with cancer or any serious physical illness, everything changes...immediately. Decisions on treatment must be made, family members need to be notified, finances become a concern, and questions of death come to the forefront. Priorities come sharply into focus. Emotions surface, sometimes powerfully.

My job has been to assist patients through the subconscious emotional mine fields that come up during cancer treatment. Some want healing, both emotionally and physically. Some want to connect to their God. There are those that I must prepare for death. At times, I've seen nothing short of miracles; at other times, I've seen people go very quickly. Working with cancer patients has shown me the resilience and frailty of life. I'm constantly reminded who is in charge: the Divine.

Cancer patients are some of the most remarkable people I've ever met. Survivors of a life-threatening illness will be forever changed. Whether they seek therapy or not, those who recover go through an enormous internal transformation. With a massive amount of courage, they face their darkest demons.

I've noticed one common subconscious theme among several cancer patients. It concerns issues around unworthiness and lack of love, but at a whole new level. As mentioned above, many of us have emotional charges concerning unworthiness because there wasn't enough love to go around in childhood, even in the midst of a loving family. Some cancer patients have experienced a lack of love not only through circumstances, but also through actuality. They simply were not loved as children; they weren't wanted. The realization of that truth can be a very bitter pill to swallow.

I've also noted parallels of those who survive cancer. Many have a very positive attitude and a willingness to be involved in their recovery. Some see cancer as the best thing that ever happened to them because it brings wonderful new people into their life. Others view it as a wake-up call, teaching them what is really important. Many learn about healing, and some connect to the Divine.

I've seen too much success to doubt the connection between the subconscious mind and illness in the physical body, especially when it comes to cancer. When forming a comprehensive plan for the treatment of a life-threatening disease, it's an extremely good idea to incorporate the healing of a potential contributing factor: the subconscious mind.

Resistance — The Divine Roadblock

A friend of mine once told me, "There are two kinds of people in this world, those who say 'I can' and those who say 'I can't.' And ya know what? They're both right." No, can't, won't, and don't are the key words of the universal energy barricade, the words of resistance.

Resistance is fear that expresses itself in terms of rigidity, closed mindedness, inflexibility, intolerance, refusal to change, excessive control, and opposition to growth. It produces an internal freezing up that you can actually feel in your body. In severe cases, I've seen it immobilize people in the form of arthritis. Resistance requires substantial energy to maintain.

Would you like to know how to cut off your connection to the Divine? Resist something — or better yet, resist everything. The more you emotionally shut off your interaction to the flow of life, the more your connection to Divine intervention will be repelled. Nothing puts the fire to spiritual awakening out quicker than resistance. It's the number one roadblock to the work I do.

The opposite of resistance is allowing, surrendering, and letting go. It's also an internal experience you can feel. It's born of relaxation and welcomes in the flow of life, fostering a fluid connection to the Divine that is constantly evolving, creating, and changing. It's a willingness to be open.

Overcoming resistance takes courage and a strong resolve to stand up in the face of your own fear. Standing up to fear, even just one time, allows you to understand that it's only fear. It's an emotional smokescreen based on past events, things that don't even exist. The more you step through it, the weaker its grip, and finally one day, it's gone.

Stress

The twentieth-century buzzword was definitely stress. The beauty of the twenty-first century is that we've perfected stress with technology. Because many of us lead such busy, fast-paced lives, we often don't even recognize how much chronic stress we're under.

Life is full of inherent stresses. If it's not one thing, it's another. It's been well documented that stress does nasty things, like creating or enhancing physical illness, as well as accelerating the aging process. Plus, connecting to a higher Divine power, especially in the early stages of a spiritual awakening, usually comes through a state of relaxation. When we're under perpetual tension, it's very difficult to establish that link.

To get a handle on the problem, let's boil stress down into two basic categories: avoidable and unavoidable.

Unavoidable stress is the product of life circumstances; the unexpected occurs, traffic grinds to a halt, we raise kids, deadlines get moved up, we relocate, workloads increase, a family member dies, life happens, etc., etc., and so on. There's not much we can do about this type of stress. The only thing we can control is how we deal with it. There are all sorts of ways to alleviate such pressures, such as meditation, recreation, exercise, hobbies, talking to friends, dealing with a problem directly, or even some type of therapy.

Avoidable stress is anxiety we can do something about. I've seen people running around like chickens with their heads cut off just because they're reacting to some kind of conditioning or mind chatter. I once knew an actor who was operating under the self-imposed deadline of attaining fame and recognition by the age of thirty. He went at it frantically and was completely stressed out. I ran into him early in his thirties and asked about his deadline. He replied, "Oh, that. That was kind of silly." Yeah, silly and nerve-racking. Sometimes we can avoid stress by simply asking ourselves, Do I really need to do this?

One of the deepest causes of stress I've witnessed, but one that rarely gets mentioned, is stress caused by not living the life you were born to live. Some of us are born knowing what we are going to do and be on this planet, but not many. Most of us have to figure it out through trial and error over decades. It's more of a journey of self-discovery. For some, the awareness of life purpose may not come together until the later stages of life. For others, sadly, it may not come at all.

As a healer, there are few things more difficult than to watch someone wrestling with the gnawing feeling that they are here for a specific purpose but don't know what it is. Or worse yet, they know what it is but don't have the courage to pursue it. They're held back by some kind of conditioning or fear they have too much to lose if they change their life course. In either case, they carry internal conflict and stress with them every day, often without realizing it. If a specific emotional charge is holding them back, that's no problem, for those can be released. However, sometimes the journey to self-purpose rests in Divine timing. In that case, the only cure is patience and trusting in a higher intelligence to lead the way to the road of discovery.

There are numerous other types of avoidable stress related to underlying subconscious emotional charge. I won't deal with these specifically. However, I will outline the mechanics necessary to release them in Lesson #3, so stay tuned.

Addictions

It came to my attention several months ago that I've been surrounded by addicts my entire life. Having been raised by alcoholics, I experienced quite a bit of pain. I spent years learning about — and healing from — the impact of addiction. With all the healing work I've done on myself, addicts still hang around on the periphery of my life. They're like subconscious projections of ghosts, reminders of what could be.

People can get addicted to anything: drugs, cigarettes, alcohol, sex, work, electronics, food. If something exists, there's an addiction for it. Addictions are generally fueled by unusually strong subconscious emotional charges. The situation increases in complexity with physical and/or chemical dependency.

In my observations, many addictions are based on a specific type of unresolved grief. Usually, it's a grief rooted in the loss of self. Somewhere in the course of living, many addicts have lost a part of themselves, as if a giant internal hole or void has been created. They use whatever available means to try and fill that abyss and bring themselves back to wholeness. Highly sensitive people seem to be particularly vulnerable. The internal hole is just too much to bear, and they use anything they can to numb the pain.

On the other hand, some people come into this life experiencing addiction as their karma. It's their life path, up to the very end. For some, the power of addiction may be too strong to overcome their genetic or chemical predisposition. Others may have such strong emotional charges that it seems easier to die than to deal with the depth of the problem.

Relationships — Sacred Connections

We're all mirrors. Each of us is an accumulation of everyone we've ever loved or hated. They have all taught us something about ourselves. They've created a response, shaping us into what we are today. We have bits and pieces of each of them inside. If you don't like something about someone, it's really only something you don't like about yourself. If you admire something about someone, it's part of you that has yet to develop.

Since life is a reflection of our own subconscious projections, then people we pull into our lives are manifestations of our subconscious, good or bad. Intimate relationships are no exception. In fact, they exponentially magnify the concept and can steer us into the Divine. Let me explain.

The way to the Divine is primarily through the subconscious mind, facilitated through states of deep relaxation. The only obstructions that stand in the way are subconscious emotional charges. Any close relationship will be a vehicle to bring those charges up. Because the relationship is close, the opportunities to expose the charges will be many. Each time a charge presents itself, there is an opportunity for healing, for removing obstacles that prevent Divine connection. As healing occurs, Divine connection increases. Therefore, in the context of healing, close relationships are sacred.

Wow! That was a mouthful. Let me put it another way: You marry your subconscious, which is the road to the Divine.

It's easy to determine when an opportunity for healing and growth in a relationship is being missed. One or both of the parties will fall into the blame and defend ritual. If someone is blaming the other for their own charge (i.e. anger, sadness, etc.), then it's very difficult for healing to occur. Remember, suffering is never about the other person. Your feelings are your feelings. Other people are just helping you experience emotions that need healing. They are props in your own subconscious play.

Lesson #2 — Homework

For the most part, emotional charges are generated in the subconscious mind and filtered through the body. You can actually feel them. Let's do a simple exercise.

Close your eyes and imagine you're in a situation where there is conflict. It may be with your spouse, children, parents, employer, neighbor, or colleagues. Or it may be a situation regarding love, health, finances, the law, business, authority, or failure. Pay close attention to where you feel the sensation associated with this conflict in your body.

Next, try to describe that emotional charge with a word or two. It may be something like this: "When I think of my father, I feel intense anxiety in my stomach" or "Whenever I think of the struggle I have with my spouse over money, I feel a heavy sadness in my heart."

Do this for every area of conflict in your life and write them down. Do you notice any differences or similarities?

Lesson #3
Awareness Leads to Healing

Hey, This Stuff Works!

So far, we have gained awareness on the nature of suffering and learned that we can actually feel subconscious emotional charges in our bodies. Now comes the good part. Let's dive into the subconscious mind and get rid of these pesky charges. This is where we leave the conceptual behind and move into the world of experience, the foundation of learning spiritual skills.

Preliminary Tips — A Healing Heads-Up

Responsibility — The Karmic Rubber Band

Remember how I said subconscious emotional charges are not your fault? Well, that's true...sort of. It turns out that the creation of subconscious charges is not your fault. However, once you have them, they're all yours, and so is the responsibility for dealing with them. Nothing will heal unless you take the necessary steps to seek that healing. That requires awareness and effort on your part, not only to heal yourself, but also to prevent the future suffering of others.

In the natural world, there are certain laws referred to as the Laws of Physics, universal and unchangeable principles on how the physical world works. The spiritual world is no different, and there are a number of unchangeable Spiritual Laws. One such law is the Law of Karma. Karma is the law of energetic cause and effect that asserts, "What you sow is what you reap" or "What goes around comes around." Once we've entered into the world of awareness, perpetuating suffering with that consciousness is a bad karmic no-no. In other words, don't hurt anybody on purpose; it will eventually come back to visit you with same strength in which it was put out. Every Napoleon has his Waterloo.

Getting Help — Synergy and Healing

The subconscious mind is a big and mysterious place. Negotiating the terrain can be a daunting task, especially if you're in pain. There will also be times when healing can seem overwhelming, or on occasion, we just get stuck. Some of the most difficult times in our lives are when we forget or refuse to ask for help. However, none of us have to go it alone. In fact, healing is much more effective and swift with support.

Synergy is the fusion of energy that creates a result where the total is greater than the sum of the parts. It applies to countless situations in life and is especially true in healing. When someone helps you through the emotional liberation process, results seem to amplify 100 times over. Who can you turn to for help in subconscious healing? There is help out there! Practitioners specializing in this unusual world include energy workers, spiritual healers, shamans, sound healers, hands-on healers, hypnotherapists, and intuitives, to name a few.

Talk Therapy and Psychology

Before we get started in subconscious healing, I'd like to briefly mention healing and traditional counseling. First off, I'm not a psychologist. However, when I started in this work, I thought it was very necessary to have a firm psychological grasp on any problem to facilitate subconscious healing. In over two decades of doing this work, my views have reversed about 180 degrees.

Talk therapy can be an invaluable tool on the road to healing. It just plain feels good to talk through and intellectually process difficult life issues. Hashing problems out verbally can lead to insights and awareness surrounding behavior, family dynamics, self-discovery, and spiritual growth. However, talk therapy is limited to the conscious mind; it rarely delves into the extent of the subconscious. People can talk themselves silly and analyze situations to death but never get to the depth of permanent healing, as if they're hitting a wall...and in essence, they are. It's called the critical faculty of the mind (remember that from Lesson #1?). Deep and lasting healing is not likely to occur until we bypass the critical faculty and enter the depths of the subconscious.

Divine Timing and the Blink of an Eye

How do you know if you have subconscious emotional charges? You don't...until they come up. As far as I can tell, the timing behind healing is driven by a much higher intelligence than you or me. You can have faith in this intelligence or not, as that really doesn't matter. Things come up when they come up. When it's time, it's time.

Some emotional charges can lie dormant for years and present themselves when it's least expected (or wanted). The funny things is, even after years of sleeping, recurring charges will have the thumbprints of the past all over them. You may find yourself saying, "I can't believe this is happening again!"

When a charge presents itself, it is as if that charge is saying, "Hey! Here I am again. Don't ignore me this time. It's time to let me go!" They want to be healed! If you don't pay attention, like Arnold warned, they'll be back — only the next time, they'll be bigger and much harder to ignore. They might even bring their friends. Since they won't be going away permanently on their own, you might as well deal with them as they come up. There's no time like the present. Keep reading to find out just out how to deal with them…so that you can give them one final, "Hasta la vista, baby."

If emotional charges seem big, nasty, countless, and undefeatable, fear not and don't lose heart. All charges boil down to a few "core" issues. In other words, no matter how overwhelming your situation may seem, you don't have that many issues to deal with, maybe only one or two, or at the very most, a handful.

Surprisingly enough, because subconscious healing happens in a state of deep relaxation, it's not as difficult as you may think. In a way, it's effortless once you learn how. As your experience increases, you'll discover that healing actually occurs in the blink of an eye. Furthermore, as healing continues, charges will decrease in intensity and frequency until eventually they're gone entirely. That spells freedom.

Delving into the Subconscious

Dreams — Off to La-La Land

Most of us have already had firsthand experience with the subconscious through our dreams. In fact, we dedicate nearly one-third of our lives to the subconscious when we sleep at night. A very common first question I ask new clients is, "Do you dream at night?" If they say yes, I know success in our work together is likely because they're already familiar with the subconscious world.

You can actually work through emotional issues in your sleep. Before dozing off tonight, think of an area in your life where you would like to see improvement. Next, while very relaxed, simply ask your subconscious to bring healing to that area. Then go to sleep. Your only job is to remember your dreams and pay attention to the messages. The easy way to remember dreams is to have a pen and paper handy on your nightstand and write them down as soon as you wake up.

Relaxation — Keys to the Divine's Car

Remember this from high school?

Kid: "Hey, Dad, can a have the keys to the car?"

Dad: "Sure, son. Here you go." (Tosses Kid the keys). "Don't be out too late."

Kid: (Bending over backward, staring at the sky with a beaming grin.) "SWEET! Thanks, Pop!"

Relaxation is the key to a Divine Cadillac heading down the highway of endless spiritual adventure. It's the portal to Divine mystery. However, to start the engine, you must first get your hands on the key. You can't go anywhere without it.

If you're thinking, Ahhhh...relaxation is a tall, cool drink with warm sun on an endless tropical beach, that's a nice start, but I encourage you to try thinking a little deeper. When I refer to relaxation to facilitate subconscious healing, I'm talking about going into a trance or meditative state. Believe it or not, this is actually a normal state of mind that everyone enters at least twice a day: right before falling asleep and just before waking up. It's the half-awake/half-asleep state of awareness, commonly referred to as the suspended dream state.

If we are to gain the full benefits from this natural suspended dream state, we need to develop and utilize it. Relaxation, like any skill, must be learned and takes practice. The deeper you learn to go, the more dynamic and effective your experiences will be. However, once the experiences start rolling in, the practice is something to eagerly anticipate and look forward to every day. It involves settling into a pleasant encounter.

Even though relaxing is a skill, it's important to mention that there's not much to it. Simply find a quiet, comfortable place to sit or lie without distraction: no kids, no phones, no noises, and no interruptions. Put on some soft music or a relaxation CD, listen to Nature, or just be in silence. If you like, burn a candle, essential oil, or incense. Create the mood. Then sit and close your eyes, breathing gently. If your mind wanders, just let it and bring your attention back to your breath. Or you can watch your thoughts drift by like clouds. Next, just let go and drift into the experience. There! You're relaxing.

The Imagination — Pretend like It's First Grade

Here's where things get interesting. In subconscious healing, the suspended dream state can be extended for a given length of time. In therapeutic situations, it lasts around thirty to forty-five minutes. When deeply relaxed in this condition, the critical faculty of the mind (remember that?) lets down, and the subconscious mind opens up. The amazing revelation is that the conscious mind is also active. You're actually subconsciously and consciously aware at the same time! It can be a mind-blowing experience the first time around, and it certainly isn't boring or usual. It opens a very dynamic internal world where emotional and visual states can be extremely amplified. This includes feelings, memories, colors, physical sensations, sounds, smells, perceptions, beliefs, and intellectual information.

When I was in first grade, we did an activity called "Eight Boxes." We simply took our big piece of construction paper and folded it once, twice, three times and — *voilà* — eight boxes! Next, we brandished our mighty crayons and colored variations of a particular theme (pets, toys, friends, etc.) in each of the boxes. When I got stuck, I squealed, "I don't know what to draw!" My teacher retorted, "Use your imagination!" I had no idea what she was talking about. First off, children under the age of eight are in a continual state of imagination. Telling a first grader to use his imagination is like telling a fish to be aware of water. However, I still wanted to know what she was talking about. How do you use your imagination? Good question. Herein lies the million-dollar subconscious prize.

My first grade teacher was under the misconception, like so many in her day, that imagination is for first graders. Nothing could be further from the truth. Everything born in the human world starts in the imagination, be it buildings, government policies, trips to the moon, entrepreneurial ideas, or great works of art. The imagination is the home of creativity, subconscious healing, and as we will learn, the birthplace of genuine power: the Divine.

To understand the imagination, it's very important to wrap your head around this concept: The imagination is real, albeit a different type of real than the conscious mind, and its influence is huge. It's a dream world that operates in shifting, day-dreamy mental pictures, full of symbols, colors, and fantasies. It also contains a vast array of perceptions and emotions. When visual images are combined with an emotional component, the results can be explosive.

Anything we imagine is possible, sometimes whether we want it to be or not.

In subconscious healing, the imagination can be exercised through memory, directed by suggestion, allowed to roam free, influenced by mood, color, and sound. Each application can be used to garnish maximum healing effect.

Let's imagine a young woman coming to see me because she was having a difficult time moving her life ahead. She lacked the energy to make necessary life changes. It was well past the time for her to advance her career, but she just didn't have the oomph to make it happen. This was a recurring pattern that seriously limited the quality of her life.

During the pre-session interview, I asked her what sensation she felt when she thought about her difficulty and where she felt it in her body. She described her subconscious emotional charge as "dread" and pinpointed it directly in her heart.

By reading a gentle story and putting on some soft music, I was able to guide her into a very deep state of relaxation. She imagined she was standing on a set of railroad tracks. I then asked her to bring up the feelings of dread in her heart and simply release them to the past. A flood of emotion began to release from her heart. Simultaneously, she imagined picture after picture from her past, leaving her heart and zooming down the train tracks like a runaway locomotive. The majority of the dread had vanished.

Over the next five sessions, we were able to determine that the dread she experienced was probably picked up from her mother. During pregnancy, her mother had slipped into a deep depression over complicated family matters. She most likely subconsciously absorbed her mom's dread while in the womb. As we continued our work, her dread eventually evaporated completely. Not only was she able to move on in her career, but she also found additional energy to take up an exciting new recreational activity. The foundation for change took place entirely in her imagination!

Intention, Decision, and Action

The three most powerful forces in subconscious healing are intention, decision, and action. The application of these forces will set the entire universe in motion.

I like boats, so let's use them in an analogy. Intention is the force of "what you want to do on purpose." It's like the rudder. It steers the subconscious to perform certain activities and directs it toward specific results. The better idea you have about where you want to go, the easier it is to get there. If you want to go fishing but aren't sure of the best spot, you may just aimlessly float down the river. Maybe you'll catch some fish or maybe you won't. If you know a specific fishing hole where lunkers pool up, your odds of landing a whopper go up enormously. Clarity of intention is crucial in learning to navigate and master the subconscious arena.

Decision-making is the boat engine, the power that sets the subconscious in motion. Once you make a decision, the subconscious will do everything in its means to bring it to you (emotional charges and all!). The more committed you are to a decision, the more likely it is to come to fruition. Needless to say, having a clear intention (i.e. a strong rudder) can direct the strength of the engine more effectively.

Action is the driving mechanism that takes intention and decision out of the subconscious mind and generates them in the physical world. It transforms the engine and the rudder into a nautical adventure. Without action, the best-laid intentions and decisions either get left in the garage or sink to the bottom of the ocean.

In subconscious healing, the principles of intention, decision, and action are the same. For example, with cancer patients, my intention is crystal clear: heal subconscious emotions underlying and contributing to cancer. Clients provide the decision by coming to see me for help. Together, we implement a plan of action to heal the subconscious and hopefully the physical body.

Subconscious Healing Techniques

Now it's time to get your hands dirty. This is the nuts and bolts, the specific subconscious healing tools. I've written this section as a reference that you can return to again and again, as often as necessary. Keep in the back of your mind that all these techniques can be done on your own. However, you must be in a deep state of relaxation, as that will exponentially amplify the effect. Remember: relaxation first, technique second, healing third. As you work with these techniques, you'll discover there is plenty of room to improvise and discover a process unique to you.

The Curious Mind — Feel the Charge until It's Gone

Before diving into specific subconscious healing techniques, it's important to develop the proper state of mind in regard to emotional charges. It's referred to as the Curious Mind. The Curious Mind naturally cultivates a certain level of necessary detachment between you and the emotional charge. All of a sudden, it's not your anger, hurt, depression, etc.; it's only an emotion you're experiencing. In other words, your emotional charges are not you, but are only something that's happening to you. As you will experience, this creates a beneficial space between you and the emotion — a very helpful gap that enhances the release process.

Try This: Start with a clear-cut intention to heal a specific emotional change completely. Sit or lie in a comfortable position and enter a deeply relaxed state. Next, feel the emotional charge in your body, as related to the area of life you're trying to heal. It may be rage in your head, heaviness in your heart, tension in your stomach, etc. It should come readily. If it doesn't, just pretend you can feel it (remember, imagination is real, so pretending works). If you get bombarded with mind chatter or distracting thoughts, just let them come and go, like watching clouds drifting by in the sky.

Next, simply pay attention to the charge as you experience it. Be curious. Say to yourself something like, "Oh, isn't that interesting. I feel rage in my head. How curious." As you focus on that experience, you'll begin to feel a weakening, softening, or letting go of the emotion.

Now, here's where everyone begins to differ, so you'll need to develop your own method of experiencing and releasing charges. You may feel the emotion as it begins to spin or swirl and move out of your body. It may start to dissolve or let go. It may create interesting sensations in your body like tingling, warmth, or deep peace. Whatever happens, keep your focus on what's taking place. Don't wallow in the emotion, but stay with it until it's gone.

That's it! Subconscious emotional charge gone. If it returns, it will come back with less intensity and less frequency. If that happens, just go through the process again. It's like lighting a log on a fire: Keep burning it until it's nothing but ash.

Flower or Sacred Object — General Emotional Release

Sometimes when using the Curious Mind approach, charges get stuck. They just won't go away. You end up flailing and wallowing in unwanted emotion. It can be a very frustrating experience. However, we have help. After all, it is the subconscious mind, and we can imagine whatever we want to come to our aid. The Flower or Sacred Object is a technique I've used countless times on clients, with immediate, successful results. Here's how it works:

Try This: While relaxed and feeling your subconscious emotional charge, imagine a beautiful flower or some sacred object hovering above you. Let it be big and powerful. Feel its presence. Recognize the fact that it has enormous healing powers and actually pulls emotional charges out of your body. At this point, you don't have to do anything! Let the flower or sacred object do all the work by pulling the charge out of your body. Keep your focus on the process until it's finished.

Age Regression — Discovering the Root Cause

It's not always necessary, but there are times when finding the root cause of a problem can produce enormous therapeutic benefit. Age Regression is a detective's approach to subconscious healing. It requires a bit of digging around but can be an extremely effective tool.

Try This: Start by relaxing deeply. When you've identified the emotional charge of interest, imagine yourself going back in time to the first time you experienced it. Again, if nothing comes to mind, just pretend. When you get there, ask yourself, "Is this a new feeling or a familiar feeling I've felt before?" Trust your answer. If the answer is, "I've felt it before," continue to go back in time. Repeat the process until the answer is, "This feeling is new." You may end up somewhere you never expected, like in your crib, your mother's womb, or someplace that makes no sense. Don't worry about the details; just trust the process. At this point, use the Curious Mind, the Flower Technique, or release the emotion back to the perpetrator. The technique doesn't matter; just stick with it until the emotion is gone.

Past Life Regression — Deeper Root Causes

Past life regression can be used to expose possible root causes to situations when everything else fails. Sometimes the source of difficulties can be quite mysterious, and delving into a past life experience can provide a new perspective to reframe healing. Plus, past life regressions can be very interesting...and a lot of fun.

Try This: Follow the steps for an Age Regression, as listed above, except let your imagination drift directly into a past life.

Self-Forgiveness — Unloved and Unworthy (It's Not Your Fault)

This is probably the most powerful technique I've come across. It can mend and fill an eternal abyss of feeling unloved. Reaching very deep, it can transform an entire life of suffering.

Try This: Settle into a meditative state. Imagine yourself going back into time, just before your conception. You have no body, and you are nothing but energy. You're about to be conceived in an act of absolute unconditional love between two people who are the embodiment of that love. Sink deeply into the experience that as you grow in the womb, your arrival is eagerly anticipated. People are excited! You are wanted!

Imagine you are born into the arms of a perfect parent. It can be someone you make up or an actual person you know. Feel unconditional love exuding from them like sunshine. Have them look deeply into your eyes, connecting heart to heart, and hear them say, "It's not your fault. It has never been your fault. It will never be your fault." Sink into the experience fully. Don't just hear the words, but receive the impact of that unconditional love into your psyche. Take it in deep because this sensation can lead to a very positive, life-changing transformation.

Forgiveness — It's Not Their Fault

Forgiveness, in this context of subconscious healing, is a little different than the human virtue. I'll discuss the importance of that in Lesson #5. Here, let's focus on a technique to release a subconscious emotional charge.

Try This: Get relaxed and think of someone whom you need to forgive. Feel the emotional charge when you think of that person, and take note of where you feel it in your body. Now, imagine yourself standing somewhere: the woods, a beach, at home, or anyplace that comes to mind. Next, imagine a small child approaching you, maybe three or four years old. As the child nears, recognize that s/he is the person you need to forgive. Observe the child as vulnerable, innocent, and at the mercy of life — the same way you were when you were that age. Be aware that the child has been a victim of his/her parents' emotional charges and understand that it's not the child's fault. Sink into that experience and feel it and then let your own pain go. Use an above-mentioned technique to release your charge or just send it back to the child. Then let the child go to dissolve into the cosmos. Or, you can pick the child up and say, "It's not your fault." Feel it deeply and remain focused on the process until it has run its course.

Energy Cords — Energy-Sucking Relationships

Have you ever been around someone who drains your energy? Perhaps it's someone around whom you just cannot be yourself. It's as if they manipulate personal interaction by consuming all of your attention, time, and vitality. Chances are good that they aren't consciously aware of what they are doing; and worse yet, neither are you! However, if you ask yourself the question, "Is anyone sucking my energy?" chances are you will have to answer "Yes," and you will know exactly who it is. Furthermore, you can actually feel where the connection is in your body, as if you're attached by an invisible umbilical cord.

This zapping of energy happens on a subconscious level and is essentially an unbalanced give and take of the life force. Left unchecked, it can lower your personal vitality, create mental fatigue, and affect your physical health. But it's easy to let it go, my friend!

Try This: Drift down into a meditative state. Allow yourself to feel the location in your body where the energy-sucking umbilical cord is attached. It may be in your stomach, back, forehead, or another area. With intent, simply allow the cord to release. Send it back to where it came from, whether you are aware of where that is or not. Feel it leaving. Next, call back all of the energy you've inappropriately given away to anyone else. Feel that energy come back into your body. Imagine the location where the umbilical cord was attached. Allow it to heal, leaving no way for any energy-sucking cord to reattach. Drift back up into the conscious world. You should be able to noticeably feel the difference.

I've used this technique countless times in healing sessions with consistent positive results. What normally happens is that the dynamic of the energy-sucking relationship will change; even if it doesn't change, the energy drain will still be gone. When I tried this technique on myself, two weeks later, the person I was having trouble with moved to another city.

Sub-Personalities — Internal Conflict and Indecisiveness

We're all made up of subconscious parts, of internal sub-personalities, if you will. There's a separate part of us in charge of every aspect of our lives, be it relationships, finances, careers, families, health, spirituality, and so on. Whatever aspect we are concerned about, there is a corresponding sub-personality. We can interact with these individual parts to gain deeper levels of wisdom into healing our bodies, psyche, and circumstance. This technique allows us to break down our subconscious into workable and well-defined components.

Try This: For the sake of example, think of a woman who is trying to decide if she should marry the man she has been seeing for a year. She loves the man for his many sterling qualities; however, he comes from a working-class family, while she comes from an established background of doctors. Thus, she suffers from a painful internal conflict of love vs. money.

There are two approaches she can use with this technique, both starting in a state of deep relaxation. First, she can imagine a sage or some other wise person who is in charge of making the decision. She then allows that sub-personality to guide her in the decision-making process. She can openly dialogue, ask questions, and get information that will lead her to a comfortable conclusion.

Second, she can imagine two sub-personalities. The first is the one in charge of the love relationship, while the second is charge of her finances. She can present her internal conflict to the two entities and allow them to discuss the situation, weighing in on all the possible alternatives and consequences. All she has to do is observe the discussion and feel the conflict in her body. The discussion ends when a resolution for her internal conflict is reached. She may marry, she may not, or she will have a viable solution that she did not consider before. In any case, a decision is made, and the tension is resolved.

Internal Guide — Assistance and Protection

In the subconscious and spiritual realms, there is help and protection readily available and at our disposal. All we need to do is ask and be aware. I've seen enormous breakthroughs in healing once an internal guide or helper arrives on the scene. Even though they are seemingly just constructs of the imagination, I have no doubt that they are somehow real. None of us are really ever alone.

Try This: After situating yourself in deep relaxation, simply imagine a guide or helper coming to your aid. Feel their presence. It may come in the form of a religious figure like Jesus or Buddha, a guardian angel or beloved ancestor, or perhaps in the form of an animal, color, or physical sensation. Whatever form it takes, learn to interact with it. Ask it for help and develop a line of communication. Then, after requesting help, pay close attention to the results in the days ahead.

Direct Dialogue — Enhance Healing, Generate Insight

In the subconscious, it's sometimes possible to communicate directly with an illness or relationship difficulty. In this technique, simply talk to the illness or person involved in order to gain insight and heal the subconscious emotional charge. Ask what needs to be done in order to heal the situation. This technique is useful when it's not possible to physically talk to the perpetrator involved. Situations may include dialoguing with body parts or dealing with someone who has died or moved away.

Try This: Let's consider the case of someone suffering with unresolved grief over a recently passed spouse. Get nice and relaxed. Use your imagination to call up a mental image of your spouse. Feel his/her presence as if s/he is actually in the room. Open a dialogue and say whatever it is you need to say to each other to bring healing and peace. You can speak out loud or to yourself. Take as long as you like and feel whatever you need to feel. Hold nothing back! Allow the conversation to run its course.

Catching the Tiger by the Tail — Overwhelming Charges

There are times in life when everything seems to stop. This could result from unemployment, an injury, or when the kids have grown and moved out. Suddenly, you're all alone with nothing to do, no distractions. There's no one there but you. Uh-oh! It's just you with you, and you have to deal with yourself. And wouldn't you know it: That's when the tiger shows up.

What is "the tiger"? It is an incredibly strong subconscious emotional charge that has been suppressed for a long time. Like an actual tiger, it can be big and scary. It can come with such force and strength that it might be completely overwhelming, maybe more than you can handle.

I've got some news, though it's not all good. Sometimes the techniques I've laid out above don't work, especially when the tiger arrives. I know what you're thinking: Great! So what do I do then? That's easy. You just grab the tiger by the tail and let it devour you. Huh? It may sound ludicrous, but please allow me to explain.

You absolutely must step into the emotion and let it take you body, mind, and soul. Remember, though, that if you choose to step into the tiger's den, be sure to do it with the intention of healing the charge completely. It takes a lot of guts because you will have to stand up to your greatest fears. You won't know what's going on or how it will turn out. Plus, this is no quick fix. The process can last up to a few days. It takes faith and trust in the releasing process.

Not too long ago, I went through a divorce. I couldn't believe it. It was my second time, and it happened under an almost identical set of circumstances as the divorce eighteen years prior. I was completely dumbfounded. Not only that, but an enormous, recurring emotional charge also insisted on surfacing. It was all about rejection. I'd experienced strong emotions before, but nothing like that, and it was more than I could deal with. It was, for lack of a better word, huge.

I could feel the charge rise up through my body, seizing my heart and cutting off my air passage. My heart rate went through the ceiling, and I couldn't breathe. It continued to expand through my entire body and felt like crystallized glass just beneath the surface of my skin.

The tiger had arrived, and I had a choice to make. I could have shaken it off, but I knew it would return at a later date, so I stuck it out with the intention of releasing the charge completely. I grabbed the tiger's tail and let it gobble me up.

What happened next was really bizarre. As this overwhelming emotion continued to capture my entire body, I experienced an amazing shift in perception. It wasn't something I did; rather, it just kind of happened. I suddenly realized that this mind-boggling emotion wasn't mine at all; it was just something I was experiencing. Instead of feeling devastating rejection, I felt like I was on a rollercoaster ride named rejection. There was an instantaneous separation between me and the feeling. As I was trying to figure out what the heck was going on, the emotion rose up and out of my body, exploding into a thousand tiny pieces like a shattered chandelier. I was exhausted but I was at peace. And just like that, the emotional charge was released.

I've heard other people describe similar experiences. Some have referred to the release as fireworks leaving the body; others have likened the experience to a volcano or the Yellowstone mud pots. Whatever the analogy, grabbing the tiger's tail allows for an incredible release of emotion from the body and the energy field.

Other Emotional Release Techniques – More than One Way to Heal

Every time I turn around it seems like someone has come up with a new technique to release subconsciously repressed emotion. Some of the methods I've run across include EFT (Emotional Freedom Technique), Body Talk, and the Emotion Code. Instead of entering the subconscious through deep states of relaxation to release negative emotion, these techniques access the subconscious mind through the physical body. Each technique has its merit; they're all valid and can be extremely effective in healing. If what I've laid out here doesn't work for you, I highly recommend checking out one of the techniques listed above. The bottom line is to alleviate pain and suffering. Use what works best for you.

Results of Subconscious Healing Work

How Do I Know if It's Working?

What does healing look and feel like? That's a good question. After all, we're not just doing this for entertainment. First and foremost, suffering stops. Your intended areas of healing improve. Anxiety attacks go away, relationships mend, problems with money vanish, health recovers, and awareness increases. In short, you feel better, and your life improves in very tangible and obvious ways, inside and out.

However, those are not the only benefits. When the subconscious mind is directed to heal, it can respond in abundance in the form of side benefits. Unrelated areas of your life may begin to improve, creativity can be enhanced, or people around you may begin to heal. Subconscious healing is a win-win situation for everyone, radiating outward from the person who is healed. The following are some results you may experience:

Coincidences, Synchronicity, and "Magic"
When directing the subconscious with healing techniques, it goes to work right away. It will begin to gather and align external events and circumstances in your physical world. It's not uncommon to experience phenomenal synchronicity.

Synchronicities are coincidences that can't be explained by mere chance. Sometimes they seem like miracles or magic. The reason they are viewed that way is because the dynamics of the subconscious aren't always recognized or understood.

Let me give an example of a theoretical elderly client. This lady came for healing sessions because she was approaching the age when people begin to look back on the events of their life instead of looking forward. She wanted to heal her relationship with her daughter, whom she hadn't spoken with for over ten years. We used the technique where she spoke with her daughter directly, during relaxation. The session went well, and she left feeling quite relieved. Three days later, guess who phoned her. If you said "Her daughter," you'd be right!

Your Condition Improves or Intensifies — Stirring the Pot
Here's a fairly common scenario: After the first session, a client may say to me something like, "After that session last week, everything got worse. I got in a huge fight with my boyfriend, my computer crashed, and I got sick." At that point, I have to explain, as convincingly as possible, why the client needs to stick with it. Healing has begun in earnest and what has happened is actually a very good sign. We just stirred the pot. Sometimes things get worse before they get better. Using the analogy of a Yellowstone mud pot, a big bubble of nasty-smelling gas just bubbled up to the surface and popped. It's bad for a moment, but the long-term effects are good. If she continues with her healing process, negative symptoms will start to disappear.

One the other hand, just the opposite can happen. Some people feel immediate relief from issues that have been plaguing them for decades. Occasionally, miraculous breakthroughs will happen right off the bat. You just never know. In either case, the result is the same: Healing has begun.

Unresolved Situations Present Themselves
Once the pot gets stirred, it's not uncommon for unresolved issues to bubble to the surface, sometimes immediately. This is the way the subconscious mind tests out the healing. It gives you the chance to respond differently by sending the message, "Okay. I get it. You can stop now."

Consider a guy who has had problems with authority his entire life. He knows it stems from his relationship with his stepfather, but even in his adult life, episodes of conflict continue to arise. It has caused him problems in school, at work, and even one small brush with the law.

Somehow, he learns his pattern may have something to do with his subconscious, so he tries a subconscious healing technique. He decides on the flower technique and actually feels "conflict with authority" release from his stomach.

Three days later, he gets a parking ticket and arrives just as the officer is placing the ticket on his window. Normally, he'd challenge the officer and start shooting off his mouth. This time, though, he recognizes the repeating pattern. In terms of healing, two possible scenarios are likely to unfold. First, he just doesn't feel the charge anymore and does nothing. Second, he feels the same desire to get involved in a conflict, but he chooses not to respond, sending the message to his subconscious that the charge is finished.

The Indictor List — Look Ma! It Works!
One of the most frustrating situations I continually ran into when I first started in subconscious healing work was when people got better. Why is that a problem? Because they commonly failed to recognize that the healing was related to our sessions! If someone comes to see me for anxiety attacks, for example, a week may pass without an attack. Then another week goes by, and then a month. A year later, they're sitting in a coffee shop and it dawns on them they haven't had an anxiety attack since that healing session a year ago. "Gee. I guess that really worked." No kidding.

Subconscious healing has a cause-and-effect component to it. If the intention is to heal something and some effort is put into it, chances are that healing will occur. It's not rocket science, folks.

Following is a list of indicators that may occur as subconscious healing begins. It took me about twelve years of observation and practice to put this list together. It is my hope that you will recognize healing not only in your area of concern, but in other areas as well.

- ○ Emotional symptoms disappear or increase (depression, anxiety, phobias, etc.).
- ○ Feelings become amplified (love, anger, happiness, sadness, etc.).
- ○ Physical ailments are relieved or worsen.

○ Senses are heightened (vivid colors, sharp hearing, sensitized touch).
○ You get physically sick.
○ Outlook on life improves (e.g., you feel happier).
○ Energy and enthusiasm increase.
○ Confidence expands.
○ Focus in life direction improves.
○ Life makes sense (e.g., you feel like your life has purpose).
○ Mental clarity increases (e.g., you know what to do).
○ Relaxation and wellbeing are increased (less stress).
○ Creativity increases.
○ Dreams become vivid or meaningful.

Lesson #3 — Homework

Get nice and cozy and set the mood for some deep relaxation. Put on some music or use my relaxation CD. Drift into a deep trance and release a subconscious emotional charge with one of the techniques used in this chapter. Feel the charge release from your body. Repeat this process for as many consecutive days as you feel the need. Try different techniques. Keep a journal of what happens, and watch for shifts in your external life in the days to come.

After about five days, use the above indicator list and see if you can check any items off. If you can, the process is working, so keep at it!

Lesson #4
Healing Leads to Awakening

Wow! They Never Taught Me This in School!

What Is God?

Not too long ago I had the opportunity to speak at a dialogue dinner. The question posed to me was, "What is God?" I was given the topic weeks in advance, so I had plenty of time to prepare. The cunning answers and slick one-liners I arranged were so craftily concocted that I was confident I could bring even the most devout atheists to their knees.

About an hour before the presentation, I was relaxed and dreaming of a time when I'd gone snorkeling in Hawaii. I was floating in a sea of tranquil, serene, colorful bliss. Then something occurred to me: Most life on this planet lives underwater. Humans have very little understanding or experience of this vast world that covers two-thirds of our planet. Then I thought of the Universe — the millions of galaxies that stretch out beyond the limitations of our imagination. Contemplating further, I realized we have five, maybe six senses to comprehend our surrounding environment, which may be infinitely larger than what we can perceive. And even beyond that, there may be infinite Universes. For all I know, there may be infinite Gods. It was a bad time to muddle my thoughts with these mental explorations, but sometimes it happens that way.

My developing belief system lends itself to a Divine Creator that has manifested everything: things we're aware of and things we are not. Minutes before the presentation I was to give, I felt like an invisible (and not very confident) grain of sand on an endless stretch of beach. So when the question was posed to me, "What is God?" I reflected, dug deep into my soul, and through the breadth of my experience I replied, "Beats me. Let's eat!"

We're humans. Thus, we're limited. How can we experience and understand the totality of an infinite Divine? We can't. We can only experience what we're capable of through our senses and the awareness of what we are. However, by being human, there are still endless worlds to explore. The physical world of the five senses is just the tip of a magnificent iceberg. Adventuring into the nonphysical realms of the human experience opens the journey exponentially. It leads to awakening to an experience of energies that are in us, beyond us, and binding us all together. Can we really experience the Divine? Of course we can — as much as we are humanly capable. Let's begin this process by exploring the world around us.

Divine Building Blocks

Nature — Expression of the Divine Subconscious

Hopefully, I've driven the point home by now that what happens in your life is an expression of your subconscious mind. The same is true for the Divine; the difference being that the manifestation of the Divine's subconscious is Nature. The cosmos, planet Earth, trees, oceans, deserts, rivers, and wildlife are expressions of Divine energy, and we are too. It's very bizarre to me that many times when we think of Nature or the environment, we don't count ourselves in the equation. We are products of this planet and of the Divine — not better or different than the puzzle itself, but a piece of that puzzle. We live here; we belong here. As we sprint into a technological future that separates us further from Nature, we tend to lose sight of that fact. We are Divine expression.

The entire Universe is a living, breathing, interactive creature, constantly in a state of flux. It operates at a pace and rhythm entirely connected to Divine energy. If you spend a few days in the wilderness away from phones, computers, motors, radios, clocks, and technology, something very spectacular will start to happen. After about the third day, things will start to change. You'll sink into a natural rhythm based solely on daylight. Mind chatter will slow, the senses will become more alert, intuition will increases, your body will relax, and the critical faculty of the mind will ease down. In short, you enter a mild and continual trance state. Your subconscious mind will be exposed to the authentic flow of the natural world (i.e., the Divine). You just...connect.

When I was younger, I devoured books about exploration. If I wasn't actually on an outdoor adventure, I was taking one in my mind. I was fascinated by stories of native cultures with a deep spiritual connection to the land and the animals. Their relationship with the Creator is born of day-to-day experience. They live it, breathe it, and eat it. For them, it isn't the conscious construct of a deity, something they learn about in Sunday school. It is real, alive...and it's available to all of us.

In 1997, I had the incredible opportunity to work as an exploration geologist on the north slope of the Brooks Range in Alaska. Our tiny nine-person village was situated at the end of an abandoned runway, about 140 miles north of Kotzebue. Welcome to Nowhere, Alaska, USA, planet Earth! We were plopped down into the middle of an arctic wilderness, its vastness defying description, a place where humans are outnumbered by grizzly bears about a hundred to one. Our three-week mission was to hike the hills in search of precious metals. I was part of an exploration team of highly trained analytical scientists, and they were very good at what they did. It was some stroke of luck for me to be recruited on such an A-Team, and this Nature boy was in absolute heaven.

As days turned to weeks in the Alaska bush, things started to change. My perception of the physical world started to shift. My sense of time adjusted to a shapeless flow of unhurried activity. Synchronicities became a daily experience. Our language modified to incorporate our surroundings, especially the weather. Body language and personal interaction became more relaxed. The ocean of land we were camped upon morphed into a living creature. Experience of the land became so surreal that it felt as if the mountains would open up and speak at any moment. The spirit of the land was tangible; we could just feel it. Drifting into a continuous state of relaxed consciousness, I was in the zone.

Toward the end of our excursion, one of the more analytical members of our team leaned over to me and said, "Hey, this is a pretty spiritual place, don't you think?" The presence of Divine energy was so strong in that untouched immensity that it managed to crack even the toughest of nuts among us.

Taking time to connect with Nature will accelerate spiritual growth. Why? Because Nature is the Divine. This doesn't mean you have to sign up for the next African safari or buy some snowshoes and trek through Antarctica. Nature is everywhere, even in the city. It's in the plants, water, weather, and sky. Take some time to get away from your car and electronic gadgetry. Slow down. Listen to the wind in the trees. Feel the sun on your face. Interaction with Nature is an excellent step to begin a spiritual awakening. It's an absolutely nonjudgmental medium that can open feelings of great depth. Nature can set the stage for powerful experiences waiting within.

Cymatics — Vibration Creates Form

When I was a senior in college, I had an incredible lucid dream that I have never forgotten. It was of a slowly spinning, pink, translucent octahedron (diamond), encapsulated within a clear sphere. The clarity of the three-dimensional geometry was fascinating. When I awoke from the dream, I could still see it in my mind. With my eyes closed, I could watch it spin for extended periods of time. I had no idea what, if anything, it meant. However, it led me to wonder if there may be some connection between subconscious geometric images and the physical world.

About ten years later, I stumbled onto a book entitled *Cymatics*, a body of research developed in the 1960s by Sir Peter Guy Manners, MD, DO, PhD, of England. The study focused on sound and vibration. In the experiments, the surface of a plate was covered with a thin layer of particles, paste, or liquid. Then, the plate was subjected to a series of vibrations, some at frequencies beyond human detection. Results showed geometric forms emerging from the material on the plates. Vibration was creating form. Being a geologist, I immediately recognized some of the geometric shapes as the crystal structures of minerals — the fundamental building blocks of planet Earth! I was captivated and remembered my dream in college. I wasn't too far off in wondering about a relationship between the physical world and something beyond the five senses. Are humans (and the entire Universe, for that matter) just physical expressions of some kind of Divine vibrational energy? Good question!

Chakras and the Human Energy Field

The answer to our question goes back thousands of years into the writings of the Vedic tradition in India (2000-600 BC), where knowledge of chakras was first unveiled. Chakras were described as centers of spinning energy, located within the human aura (energy field). There are seven main chakras, each specifically located from the base of the spine to the top of the head. These receive, assimilate, and transmit life force (Divine) energy. Each chakra contains measurable patterns of activity and reflects essential aspects of human consciousness. Thus, the seven chakras are major contributors to the subconscious human experience.

The diagram on the back of this book is a simplified map of the human chakra system. Use it as a reference with the list below, which contains the name of each chakra and its corresponding attributes.

Chakra: **First, Root**
Location: Base of the spine
Color: Red
Note: Middle C
Life Issues: Survival, grounding, organization, home, family

Chakra: **Second, Sacral**
Location: Just below the navel
Color: Orange
Note: D
Life Issues: Pleasure, sexuality, abundance, wellbeing

Chakra: **Third, Navel (Solar Plexus)**
Location: Stomach area
Color: Yellow
Note: E
Life Issues: Self-worth, self-esteem, confidence, personal power, freedom of choice, will

Chakra: **Fourth, Heart**
Location: Heart area
Color: Green, Pink
Note: F
Life Issues: Community, Nature, love, family, friendship, purity, innocence

Chakra: **Fifth, Throat**
Location: Throat, mouth, jaw, ears, and shoulders
Color: Turquoise, Blue
Note: G
Life Issues: Truth, creativity, self-expression, communication

Chakra: **Sixth, Brow (Third Eye)**
Location: Between the eyebrows
Color: Indigo, Violet
Note: A
Life Issues: Wisdom, knowledge, imagination, intuition, discernment, planning, vision

Chakra: **Seventh, Crown**
Location: Top of the skull
Color: Violet, White

Note: B
Life Issues: Beauty, harmony, spirituality, connection to
the Divine (life force) energy

There's a little discrepancy over the exact note for each chakra. The important thing to remember is that it's a gradational system. It's like a musical scale, forming a continuous spectrum from bottom to top. It's not an exact science, so there's a little wiggle room that can be compensated for with the application of intention. (Keep in mind that intention is one the most powerful forces in the subconscious mind). Therefore, it doesn't matter if healing is done on the second chakra with a D or D# tone. With the power of a specifically set intention, the subconscious can adjust and use a tone that is the closest fit to manifest healing in that area.

Keep in mind that this is only a general map and guide. The chakra system is a very fluid, dynamic, and integrated energy system. It often flows and moves like ocean waves or gentle clouds of electricity. With experience and practice, this movement can be felt inside and around the physical body. The chakras can also be influenced by sound, color, thought, feeling, and intention, all with positive or negative results.

Subconscious Emotional Charges and Chakras

Let's go back to the Lesson #2 homework for a moment. Hopefully, from that exercise, you were able to feel a subconscious emotional charge (repressed emotion) in your body. Maybe it was dread in your heart, anxiety in your stomach, or tension in your throat. Chances are it was associated with a particular chakra and corresponding life issue. For instance, dread in the heart may be related to a childhood issue regarding unworthiness or lack of love. Anxiety is the stomach may be associated with conflict and authority. Tension in the throat may be related to an inability to speak your truth.

In all the years I've been doing subconscious healing, the chakra map has held up as a fairly reliable tool to pinpoint key life issues. It seems that Divine vibration is filtered through the chakras and subconscious mind to create our experiences in life. Through no fault of our own, traumatic experiences create strong, unpleasant emotions that we unintentionally repress into the subconscious. We can feel them in our body. It's as if they get hung up or stuck on our chakras, like dirt particles on an air filter. As long as they remain there, repeating patterns (often negative) will continue to emerge in our lives until the emotion is released. In Lesson #3, we learned an assortment of techniques to let those emotions go. However, there's more than one way to wash a car, so let's learn another method for cleaning those chakras.

Cleaning the Chakras — Sound Healing

Okay, so chakras are spinning centers of electromagnetic activity in our energy field. Each chakra resonates to specific vibration in the form of sound; for example, the third chakra in the Solar Plexus resonates to the E note. That means the third chakra operates at maximum efficiency at that frequency. The Solar Plexus likes the note E, and it buzzes in E when it's healthy. Every time the pure note of E is chimed, the Solar Plexus celebrates.

Now, let's throw a subconscious emotional charge into the soup. Let's say some guy was physically abused by his father when he was young. The abuse created a repressed emotion in his subconscious mind that got stuck in his third chakra. He can feel the anxiety in his stomach every time his boss walks into the room. He knows it's related to his childhood, but he can't seem to do anything about it. In fact, it's getting worse, and he thinks he may be getting an ulcer.

His subconscious charge is out of harmony with the third chakra, and this creates anxiety in his stomach. Can sound help him? Yes! How? If the pure tone of E is chimed, the chakra will begin to resonate to that frequency. Because the stuck emotion doesn't resonate with that tone, it will essentially let go and release, restoring the harmonic frequency of the third chakra. The most effective tools to generate the necessary pure tone are tuning forks and crystal sound bowls.

Okay, so you're thinking, You're kidding, right? Playing a tuning fork for my Solar Plexus? Sounds like some kind of voodoo to me. I'd be inclined to agree, except for one thing. I've seen it work hundreds of times in healing! It's simple and direct, though it's usually not an instant fix. For most people, healing is a process. It can take repeated applications with complementary techniques to produce desired healing results. Nevertheless, sound healing can be incredibly effective. When combined with techniques learned in Lesson #3, sound healing can considerably accelerate subconscious healing.

So why don't we just go around and ding-dong everybody with sound, heal them up, and create Utopia on Earth? First off, we need to remember the critical faculty of the mind. Remember, it's the protective barrier between the conscious and subconscious mind. Sound healing increases exponentially when the critical faculty is let down. How do we do that again? By entering deep states of relaxation. So, before clanging the tuning forks, it's extremely beneficial to be in a trance. That takes time and usually some help.

There's one other thing that influences sound healing and many other types of healing modalities. It's beyond the scope of this book, but it does deserve some mention here. It depends on who is holding the tuning forks, as some people are more gifted at healing than others. It's nothing short of a Divine blessing to be assisted by someone who carries the positive vibration of genuine healing.

Cleaning the Chakras — Colored Light Healing

Colored light healing is similar in principle to sound healing. Colored light transmits frequencies that resonate with particular chakras. Healing can occur by applying appropriate colored light to the proper chakra to restore healthy harmonic frequency. For this reason, tools in your practitioner's toolbox may include colored glasses, prisms, and color wheels.

The Divine Connection — The Experience of a Lifetime

The Road to the Divine...Bumps and All

Look out! It's time for another analogy! This time, let's use a highway with the journey beginning in the conscious mind. As you approach the highway, you begin to see the corridor that contains the pavement, shoulders, median, guardrails, etc. This is the subconscious mind, and according to the map, it's the route and passageway to the Divine. At the entrance ramp is a gate that requires a toll; to drop the gate so you can get on the highway, you have to pay. This is the critical faculty of the mind, and the payment required is a deep state of relaxation. As you pull onto the highway in a trance, you notice rocks and potholes everywhere — so many you can't even see the pavement. These are subconscious emotional charges. As you work at removing the charges, you begin to reveal the pavement beneath, a dazzling, brilliant energy.

This is your first experience of the Divine. The feeling is so strong and amazing that you dive in and enthusiastically remove any charges that stand between you and the Divine. The more charges you remove, the more Divine experience you have. Soon enough, you're cruising on this amazing magic carpet of Divine energy. Emotional charges still come up from time to time, but they're easily dispatched. As you learn the ebb and flow of the magic carpet ride, life becomes more and more effortless. This is Divine flow, a continual connection with Divine presence.

Then, something funny happens. You remember you are on the road to the Divine, but discovered *the road is the Divine!* However, according to your map, the Divine should be just ahead. As you enter this place on the map, you start to feel unusual. You look out the window and sense that your physical surroundings, the events in your life, and even the people you know are attached in some way. Strangely, everything seems to fuse together: the road, the tollgate, the potholes, and things that are not even on the road. They are all separate, yet they are linked. Somehow, you grasp the notion that you're involved in generating this life experience. To clear your head and regain your senses, you look at yourself in the rearview mirror. Gazing into your own eyes, you see a flash of brilliant light. Then, a mind-blowing insight explodes into your awareness that makes sense of everything. The Divine is you!

If you're reading this book, chances are you may already be aware of this universal implication that we are co-creators of Divine will. That awareness is great, but it's not enough. We need to take it a step further to the real beginning of the journey, to make the leap from Divine belief to Divine experience. When you do so, your life will never be the same; rather, it will be permanently transformed for the better. If you choose to participate, it will be an ongoing experience of evolution — an exciting, wondrous adventure that is absolutely full of joy.

Emotional Charges and the Divine

Before learning about Divine connection, it's important to understand the role subconscious emotional charges play in helping that connection along. Wait...did I read that right? Help the connection? That's exactly right! Allow me to explain...

As we have learned, the subconscious mind is the home of repressed emotion (subconscious emotional charges). It's also the home of the Divine. Really? Doesn't it get a little crowded in there? It sure does. In fact, subconscious emotional charges are actually obstacles that get in the way of Divine connection. However, as charges are released, the Divine starts to shine through. Eventually, you will come to realize that the Divine is waiting behind each charge to help you. Then, the light goes on and you realize, emotional charges are gifts *from* the Divine. The Divine actually brings up your emotional charges so that you have to ask for help, thereby experiencing the Divine again.

A few years ago, a client of mine was looking for a new home. She wanted a place with a lovely garden so she could meditate in natural surroundings. So she sat in meditation, invoked the Divine, and asked for help. Later that very day, an exceptionally strong emotional charge came up concerning her self-worth. She asked the Divine for help and...boom! A big unresolved issue was put right in her face.

She was aware enough to recognize the charge and use a subconscious healing technique to let it go. Of course, she had to call upon the Divine again. Within a day or two, she found a beautiful little house that backed onto a wooded area — a perfect sanctuary for her.

She later told me that if the Divine hadn't brought up her charge of low self-worth, it would not have healed. If it had not healed, then her self-esteem would not have been high enough to manifest such a beautiful house. It was if the Divine set up all the circumstances to create healing, which resulted in a beautiful home, which led to a closer connection to the Divine.

Connecting with the Divine? Here We Go!

I use the term "Divine energy" to refer to a third-party energy we're surrounded by at all times. It's around us and in us. It's a natural part of being human. However, somewhere along the line, we separated from this integral part of our being. The good news is that there are ways to reestablish the connection. First, we need to learn the art of dissolving our unawareness of this incredible presence.

Initially, the best way to link up with Divine presence is in deep states of relaxation, trance, or mediation. What happens when we get deeply relaxed? The critical faculty on the mind lets down, and the subconscious mind opens up. Suddenly, we're in the living room of the Divine.

When we enter this life, we're given the gift of an enormous free will. We can do as we please for good, evil, or anywhere in between. So it goes for our ability to connect with Divine presence. When we enter the subconscious mind, we can connect with the Divine in any way we choose.

Another way to put it is to say that the Divine lives in the imagination. What?!? You've got to be joking! You mean I can just make it up? Yep! The Divine makes it easy for us. Imagine your relationship with the Divine as whatever you wish, and the Divine will respond in like manner. What that means is the way you experience the Divine is how it is. It sounds simple because it is.

If you imagine a disapproving, angry, white, male God with a beard, waiting around to nail you on judgment day, that's exactly what you're going to get. On the other hand, if you imagine a nurturing, loving, omnipotent, protective, best friend who answers all of your prayers all of the time, that's what you're going to get. So, to improve the quality of your life, it's a great idea to connect with a Divine who is extremely friendly, helpful, protective, and benevolent. The more personal, compassionate, and loyal you image the Divine to be, the more success you will have in living a happy, well-adjusted life.

If you're a visual type of person, you can imagine the Divine as a prominent religious figure, an ancestor, an animal totem, guardian angel, or color. You'll "see" the Divine in your mind. If you're more sensory, awareness of movement or physical sensation may be how you connect. You'll "feel" the Divine. Some people are more auditory and "hear" the Divine inside. The sky is the limit with Divine connection, and it's based on your imagination and whatever works best for you.

Connecting with the Divine — What's it Like?

Connecting to the Divine is different for everyone. It's personal. No one else can know what you feel, see, hear, or think or what that means to you. However, let me share some of my experiences to give you an idea. I try to do formal mediations twice a day; once when I wake, and once before I go to sleep. I don't try to clear my mind or do anything fancy. I'm a sensory person, so all I do is sit in the silence and feel Divine presence. I sink into an experience.

When I first started to become aware of Divine presence, I only recognized it as energy I could feel. I initially noticed strange swirling sensations that were not confined to the limitations of my physical body. When I focused on them, they moved inside, outside, and around, from just above my head to down around my knees. I just paid attention to them at first without really thinking about them. Years later, it was a bit of an epiphany to recognize these swirling sensations as Divine energy. In all honesty, it blew me away.

Over time, as I continued to connect with them, they started to change and grow. Simultaneously, the circumstances of my life changed considerably, to reflect the transformation that was occurring inside. Things improved, and I felt more like myself. At this point in my life, this energy feels like mild electricity that comes out of my hands, feet, heart, and the back of my neck. My relationship with Divine energy has grown.

Your experience will be different. It will be up to you to recognize your Divine connection and to take steps to expand that connection. Connecting to this energy on a regular basis is the first step to creating wonderful life renovations.

Knock, Knock! It's the Divine — What to Expect

Once you start to connect with the Divine, a variety of shifts will take place. For some, it happens very quickly and to great extremes, while for others it may be slow and gentle. In the beginning, these are some things you can expect to happen:

- ❖ Frequent experiences of deep peace and calm.
- ❖ Unexpected feelings of happiness and joy.
- ❖ Improved relationships.
- ❖ Circumstances preventing you from experiencing the Divine are released.
- ❖ Creativity increases.
- ❖ Intuition and psychic abilities sharpen.
- ❖ Awareness increases, and sensing of energy is activated.
- ❖ Life has more meaning and purpose.
- ❖ A desire to contribute emerges; you want to give.
- ❖ Wellbeing increases (physical, financial, emotional, and spiritual).
- ❖ Healing can accelerate. Subconscious charges may come up quickly and intensely.
- ❖ Life gets more interesting, exciting, and fun.
- ❖ Synchronicities become common.

❖ Prayers get answered.

❖ Problems start to improve by themselves.

❖ Living is more effortless, and things flow.

❖ Abundance radiates. There's always enough, and your needs are taken care of.

❖ Miracles happen.

Divine Validation — Am I Deluded?

So I feel little swirlies and waves of electricity in my body. Who cares? Maybe I'm just a nutcase. Good point. But what if you think you have a connection to the Divine? Then what?

The first thing to do is trust the connection. Self-doubt is the quickest way to wipe out your Divine relationship. The next thing to do is to experiment. Try it out. Get validation. After all, what good is the Divine if you can't get a little help? In fact, ask for Divine assistance in everything. Give the Divine something to do.

To initiate Divine help, first go into a relaxed state and feel or see the Divine, whichever way works best for you. Then state your request, whatever it is. Maybe you need help with finances, perhaps your health is suffering, or maybe you are involved in a relationship that is on the rocks. Ask for help, knowing the Divine answers all your prayers. See it, feel it, and trust it, realizing the process of Divine help has already begun. Then, track your results by writing them down. Pay attention in the days ahead and expect answers to your prayers. Just be aware that sometimes answers come in ways you won't expect. Continue to ask frequently.

My Prayers Weren't Answered — What's Up with That?

On rare occasions, prayers don't get answered. There are usually a few reasons for this. First, you can't override the free will of another person. You can connect to the Divine, visualize, and pray with all your might, but if Johnny wants to be a bank robber, then that's his call; he is traveling his own road to the Divine, and you need to let it go. Second, it may just not be the right time. Possibly, you or someone else involved in your prayer or the situation needs to gain more life experience before your prayer can be fulfilled. Third, sometimes we're just not allowed to know because what we are asking for is beyond our limited view and wisdom. In this case, it takes faith. And lastly, our request isn't in alignment with Divine energy. It may be based on fear, greed, or anger. When requests out of alignment with Divine will aren't fulfilled, they usually bring up some type of subconscious emotional charge.

Oneness University — The Oneness Blessing

My first experiences of Divine energy came through Oneness University, home of the Oneness Blessing. The University is located in southeastern India, with satellite groups and campuses all over the world. The Oneness Blessing claims to transfer Divine energy from the Divine to a recipient via a trained practitioner. It's said to initiate a neurobiological shift in the brain, quieting mind chatter and permanently opening spiritual channels. The net result is a continual ability to perceive and connect with Divine energy. Based on my experience there, I can unequivocally state that Oneness University delivers the goods in abundance. For information, check out their website listed in the References section in the back of this book.

Enhancing Divine Connection

Virtues as Doorways

Now we've figured out how to connect to the amazing life force we call the Divine. Let's up the ante and enhance the Divine link by using human virtues, human qualities that boost the experience of life. Keep in mind that virtues are not the Divine in and of themselves, but they are doorways. I've listed a few below that will consistently enhance your relationship to the Divine.

Forgiveness
You can never be happy if you cannot forgive. Why? Because without forgiveness, you will become a slave to the subconscious emotional charges you carry inside. In other words, if you can't forgive, somewhere inside, you will always be a victim to your own anger, hurt, or fear. Forgiveness, though, may not be what you think it is. That said, let's take a look at what forgiveness really is.

My original ideas of forgiveness were likened to the priest and the confessor. I would stand mightily and grant my absolution to my transgressors. The problem was, I was still pissed off. I've grown to understand forgiveness as a disconnection of energy. If someone has been wronged or hurt by someone, the two are connected through anger, victimhood, horror, or sadness. Forgiveness comes about when that connection no longer exists and the emotional charge has been released. That does not mean we should condone unacceptable behavior. It just means letting go of a negative relationship.

For the sake of example, consider a couple who gets divorced because one of the spouses has an affair. The victim may be deeply hurt for years. The only way out is to release the associated emotional charge. If the charge isn't released, of course, it will repeat at some later date. How will you know when you have finally forgiven someone? Just think of them! If there is no charge, forgiveness is likely complete. With growth and awareness, you will see the situation as a learning experience. The circle will be complete when you can remember your transgressors with a heart of compassion and joy.

Gratitude and Appreciation

Genuine gratitude is like a Divine magnet that works miracles. When we utilize feelings of gratitude while invoking the Divine, the Divine seems to respond by saying, "Oh, you liked that? It must mean you want more." Gratitude can also enhance abundance. If you want to attract something into your life, focus on what you appreciate.

Let's say I have a client who is really struggling with finances. To heal this problem, the first thing we do is go into a relaxed state and ask for Divine assistance. Next, we release the emotional charge of unworthiness that she feels in her abdomen. Drifting back in time, we focus her attention on a time when she had money rolling in. At that point, she is able to deeply feel appreciation in her body and carry that forward into her vision of the future. The Divine responded immediately with a new source of income within just a few days.

Compassion

Awareness of your emotional charges will automatically lead you to the state of compassion. Once you realize you are the creator and master of your own suffering, you begin to realize that everyone else is, too. The point is, we're all in the same boat. We've suffered, we've hurt others, and we all have emotional charges. We tend to be unaware. We were programmed when we were young. Believe it or not, charges that drive me to alienate my children are similar to charges that motivate a suicide bomber to take action. Everyone has emotional charges similar to the criminal, the abuser, or the neglector. Once we begin to see how the subconscious mind works, we can understand how we're all in it together. With enough insight, we may begin to realize it's nobody's fault. It's just the way things are.

Self-Acceptance

I have had more than one client say to me, "I have so many charges that I'll never get them all out" or, "I'll never be able to stop all these negative thoughts." Both of these statements are loaded with self-judgment, which is a charge in itself. A crucial component of putting an end to suffering is self-acceptance. Accepting yourself as you are, with all of your perceived imperfections, will lead to an awakened state. When you can accept yourself, charges and all, you will begin to accept others as they are. As you grow in self-acceptance, you will begin to intermingle with Divine energy and experience yourself as one in the same. At that point, living in joy is not far off.

Self-Confidence
Surprisingly enough, when considering Divine interaction, this virtue doesn't get nearly enough credit. The Divine responds exceptionally well to self-confidence. If you intend for something to happen, make a decision, take action, and invoke Divine help, and then *think* it will happen; it may come to fruition. On the other hand, if you take all the same steps to make something happen and *know* it will happen, then it will happen. Self-confidence is a feeling in the physical body of "knowingness." It's solid, strong, and unshakeable. I've seen self-confidence produce numerous successes, especially in the world of sports. It's a key ingredient to take any game up to the next level, and applications to spirituality are no different.

One note of caution: Self-confidence without humility becomes over-confidence or arrogance. This abuse of the self-confident virtue may hold up for a while, but it will eventually alienate people or result in a crash-and-burn situation. The end result will be the unveiling of a subconscious emotional charge.

Lesson #4 - Homework

Now we're getting serious...two homework assignments! Dig yourself in for some power relaxing.

1. How to Experience the Divine

Settle yourself into a nice, deep state of relaxation. See if you can let go and drift into a deeper state than ever have before. When you're ready, simply imagine the Divine coming to you. It may come in the form of a vision or a physical sensation. Trust whatever form it chooses and change it to your liking, if necessary. Go into the experience as deeply as you can without using any effort. Stay with it until you feel like you have had enough.

Return to the experience frequently, daily if possible. Learn to communicate with the presence and ask it for help regularly. Track your results.

2. Releasing Emotional Charges and the Divine

Hopefully, by this point, you've become aware of your emotional charges and have spent a little time releasing them with some success. There's one thing I forgot to mention that will accelerate the healing process immensely: Call on the Divine before using a subconscious healing technique. Incorporate a virtue such as gratitude or forgiveness to enhance the process. For starters, try the formula below. Once you get it down, it should only take a few minutes.

- ❖ Sit and relax.
- ❖ Invoke the presence of the Divine.
- ❖ Give thanks.
- ❖ Ask the Divine for help in any area of life (be specific).
- ❖ Use a subconscious healing technique until your charge is gone.
- ❖ Forgive the perpetrator.
- ❖ Ask for forgiveness from the perpetuator.
- ❖ Forgive yourself.
- ❖ Thank the Divine.

Lesson #5
Awakening Leads to Development

Toto, I've a Feeling We're not in Kansas Anymore

Disclaimer

Here's where we divert from the textbook style of this manuscript. Some of what lies ahead can't be taught; it just happens. As your spirituality opens up, mystical encounters will occur. It's unavoidable. The best way I know to prepare you for what may come is to share stories of experience. The narrative ahead is full of actual events encountered by me or people I know. It's time to leave the hypothetical behind.

Remember, spirituality is about improving the quality of life in order to live a normal happy existence. However, as you develop your connection to the Divine and dive deeper into the spiritual swimming pool, strange and marvelous things will start to happen. These mysterious events are not the central theme of spirituality, and placing your focus there can really get you sidetracked. That said, buckle your seatbelt and prepare for the ride of your life! This is where spirituality gets incredible, weird, bizarre, dangerous, outlandish, exciting, and downright fun!

Divine Experience — The Mystical and Surreal

In the Beginning — It's Okay...I Promise You're Not Going Nuts

Congratulations! I'd like to commend you on your new friendship with the Divine. As the relationship begins to unfold and you become familiar with this presence and associated sensations, you may begin to ask for more. As the old adage goes, be careful what you ask for!

The Divine always bucks up. In the beginning of a spiritual awakening, asking the Divine for more connection and experience will certainly net results. It's as if the Divine says, "You want what? Are you sure? Okay, buddy. Here you go!"

It's not unusual to get blasted when you first open up to mystical experiences. For some, it can last for quite a while...even years. Events, people, and coincidences can start rolling in like ocean waves, one after the other. It's similar to the honeymoon phase, beginner's luck, or the excitement for a new way of life. What you're entering is a whole new perception and way of experiencing the world. It can be exhilarating, expansive, and breathtaking. If it becomes too overwhelming, ask the Divine to bring experiences in a way you can comfortably handle. Life transformation doesn't have to be complicated.

A few years ago, a friend of mine had a spiritual awakening, in spades. He read an article on guided meditation, got a wild hair, and decided to give it a try. Living in a tiny town, he was stunned to actually find a guided meditation group nearby. When he arrived, the leader of the group asked, "Why are you here?" to which he replied, "I dunno. I read an article, I guess." Being perceptive and somewhat intuitive, she asked again, "Why are you really here?" He thought about it a moment and said, "I guess I feel like I have a block to my creativity." Thinking back on that comment, he realized it was somewhat bizarre at the time because he really didn't have any creative inclinations.

While he was being guided into a trance state, the woman asked, "What does the word abandonment mean to you?" At that point, he exploded into tears of a major emotional release. An endless parade of images from his past flowed through his mind. His initial experience in the subconscious arena was very intense.

Three days later, his shaky marriage ended unexpectedly and abruptly. A month later, he was fired from a job he didn't really like. Three months later, circumstances forced him to move to a new town and begin a new life. All the while, he kept attending the group meditation, broadening his mystical experiences in the subconscious. Not until later would he discover that his experiences there were actually encounters with Divine energy.

As all this was going on, he learned to play bass guitar and ended up as a member of a pretty hot band. He began to paint. Eventually, some of his work showed up in a New York City art gallery. At the same time, he cranked out a couple of books and began woodworking. Divine energy was surging through him, seeping out all over the place. The last time we met, he seemed genuinely happy. All he needed was to let go of everything that had stood between him and his irrefutable destiny.

Delusion — It's not Okay...You ARE Going Nuts

Listen. Do you hear that sound? Shhh...Listen closely. It's the echo of The Twilight Zone theme music...Nee-ner, nee-ner...Nee-ner, nee-ner...Nee-ner, nee-ner.

Woo-woo! No, it's not a train. It's the phrase some people use for New Age spirituality when it seems a bit flakey, and in some cases, rightly so. Crystals, incense, tarot cards, anything purple, psychic readings, and the aura that surround them can be very off-putting for any pragmatist anchored in the empirical world. Although these tools have their place on the stage of spiritual discovery, placing too much emphasis on the supernatural and paranormal can cross the border into delusion. The Universe is a big place, and you can get lost in it.

Negotiating the nonphysical terrain of spirituality can be a bit dicey. Sometimes there's a fine line between spirituality and psychosis. So how do you draw the line? It's simple. Spiritual events need to be verified in the physical world. Jesus healed the sick and the lame. If someone comes to me for subconscious healing regarding their anxiety attacks, then their anxiety attacks better go away. The proof is always in the pudding. If experiences of the subconscious and the imagination can't be verified in the physical world, then it should raise your eyebrows of suspicion.

Kundalini

Kundalini is the sleeping, dormant, potential force in the human energy field, stored in the root chakra. Historically it is symbolized as a coiled serpent at the base of the spine. During the process of spiritual awakening and learning to connect to the Divine, the kundalini can rise up through the chakras leading to mystical experience. Sometimes it can be extremely powerful and disorienting, especially if you don't know what's happening.

Some of the effects may include:

- ❖ Involuntary jerks, tremors, or shaking, especially in the arms and legs.
- ❖ Energy rushes or feelings of electricity circulating the body.
- ❖ Intense heat or cold, passing through the chakras.
- ❖ Visions or sounds.
- ❖ Diminished or heightened sexual desire.
- ❖ Intense emotional purging.
- ❖ Depression.
- ❖ Pressure inside the skull, often accompanied by headaches.
- ❖ Bliss, feelings of infinite love and universal connectedness.

I have a friend who went through a kundalini experience a while back. He had just split up with his girlfriend and decided to seek counseling during the grieving process. He also started meditating to relieve his anxiety. In the first meeting with his therapist, she tried to explain something to him by drawing a graph on a piece of paper. As soon as the pencil hit the paper, he felt a slow explosion of warm, brilliant energy creeping up from the base of his spine. It moved up his back and encapsulated his entire body. He told me, "I don't know what ecstasy is, but that must have been close." As he left his therapist's office, he noticed he could see everything in crystal-clear 3D. He was in a heightened state of awareness that lasted the entire day, and he drifted in and out of it over the next six weeks.

A couple days later, he was walking downtown on the sidewalk. As he passed a particular car, the alarm went off. He kept walking, and the alarm shut down when he was about thirty feet away. He thought that was rather strange, so he turned around and walked back to see what would happen. The alarm went off again and shut down when he was about thirty feet past it. Intrigued, he turned around and again walked past the car: same result. He was awe-struck. People on the sidewalk were starting to notice. A bit embarrassed and startled, he kept moving.

A block down the street, he entered a bookstore; immediately, the fire alarm went off. He scampered out of the store, and the alarm stopped. He was starting to feel a little uneasy thinking, What is happening here?!? Down the street, he entered another building. Again, the fire alarm went off, and a steel gate shot down in front of him, closing off the corridor. He was starting to freak out. Over the next two days, he continued to trip alarms and burn out lights. His electrical system was getting rewired.

During this time, he developed a very uncharacteristic relationship with a woman. It was hot and steamy, very sexual. He told me, "I don't know what's going on, but this relationship has something to do with setting off car alarms. I can feel energy surging through me everywhere. It's great!" The two of them seemed to be having the time of their lives.

He also continued with his meditations. They were coming alive, taking on lives of their own. His visions were so lucid and clear that it was like watching TV. Some pertained to his past, and some to his future. His intuitive side was unveiling with amazing accuracy. He was getting flooded with energy. The kundalini had risen!

Energy Infusions and Divine Downloads

Energy infusions are downloads of Divine energy that open the recipient to higher realms of human consciousness. They're driven by Divine timing and grace, subject entirely to the Divine's discretion. As far as I can tell, it's not possible to create these events. You can only be open to receiving them when they arrive. In other words, when they come, don't resist.

Several years ago, I went on a retreat. It was a big deal because it was a week long. Plus, it was pretty spendy. I wasn't really sure why I wanted to go, other than the fact that I had been working long and hard in northern Canada as a geologist. I needed a break.

When I decided to attend, something occurred that isn't so unusual for participants of spiritual retreats: My growth process started. Even while the event was still weeks away, parts of my life that needed healing came up with vigor. Issues in my relationship came up so strong, causing an anxiety attack that lasted nearly a week. It was a massive subconscious emotional charge. At that time, I didn't have the awareness to effectively release the charge, so I kind of beat it back with a stick and repressed it back into the subconscious. It gave me an inkling, though, that the retreat was going to be something major.

On my way to the retreat, I felt wishy-washy about going. Even though I was in the airplane, my heart was pretty noncommittal. I just wasn't into it. Apparently, that didn't sit very well with the Divine, who wanted my presence wholeheartedly or not at all. I had no way of knowing, but a defining synchronicity was one its way.

Because it required an international flight, I had to change planes at LAX. As I presented my passport to the ticket agent, she said, "We can't accept this. It has water damage. You'll have to get another one." I was livid and retorted, "What!?! Another passport? I've been using this passport for the last three years to work internationally — Canada, Denmark, and Sweden! No one has ever questioned it! You're not even an immigration official. How can you deny me entry into another county?" Unflinchingly she replied, "Sorry. Airline policy." She wasn't going to budge.

The retreat was still two days off. If I was lucky, I could get an emergency passport from the federal building in LA at Brentwood, or I could just bag it and go back home. I was sure the retreat would have refunded my money. I had a choice to make. I could make the effort or blow it off. (Remember how decision is one of the most powerful forces in the subconscious?) After whining and moaning for a while, I toughened up and decided to go. With that decision and intention established, the Divine set me up for one of the wildest times of my life...and that was only the beginning.

I fortuitously got a new passport and arrived at the retreat with everyone else. Apparently, there was a high-profile celebrity-type at the retreat. For simplicity's sake, let's call him Superman. I had never heard of him before, and when someone explained to me who he was, I replied, "Ohhhhhh..." I had never been around anyone like him. The guy was an absolute force of Nature. He could sit quietly in the corner and command everyone's attention just by his presence. He carried tons of energy. I was actually mildly annoyed he was there. I had planned on utilizing my week there to go inward, without disruption, and it seemed like Superman could be a gigantic distraction. How was I supposed to know the Divine was going to use him to help me? Superman was going to be a supreme conduit of Divine energy, assisting me in my awakening process. The weird part was, I would neither meet nor speak with Superman the entire time I was there.

On the first full day of the retreat, we were guided in meditation to experience the Divine. We were instructed to relax deeply and imagine the Divine in any way it presented itself. As I drifted in deep, guess who shows up. You got it. Superman. I couldn't believe it! I was actually kind of pissed off. I was saying inside, *C'mon! Not this. Anybody but him.* I tried to shake him off, but my imagination wouldn't let it go. He was there, bigger than life, and he wasn't going away. Deciding not to resist, I invited him in. At that very moment, the image of Superman entered my body, more powerful than a locomotive. I could feel and hear something hitting my chest so hard that I gasped for air. Superman went straight into my heart chakra and exploded.

Okay. So that was weird. Download number one.

Two days later, the theme of the day was joy. The leaders of the retreat were really bringing the juice as we entered meditation, and joy was in the air. As we collectively settled into a trance state, people started breaking out in laughter. It was hilarious. As the meditation continued, it hit me too. I laughed so hard that tears just started rolling. It was everything I could do to keep from wetting my pants.

As the laughter gradually receded, I rolled over on all fours, and my body began to uncontrollably rock from back to front. I couldn't stop it. At the same time, I felt an intense pressure encompassing the top part of my skull. I felt like a baby getting forced through a birth canal. It was incredibly intense. I hurt all over, especially around my temples. Later, I learned this is called a rebirthing experience, and it can happen at the beginning of a major life transformation.

As I imagined myself coming out of the birth canal, it felt like my crown chakra burst open with brilliant light. As I pushed through, guess who was there to greet me. That's right...Superman! I thought, *Not again*. Doesn't this guy ever give up? This time he was standing there, pointing straight at me with his arm and fingers extended, as if he had just completed a karate chop. All of a sudden, energy started streaming out of his fingers, and a wall of electricity rose up behind him and came at me like a river at flood stage. I was completely engulfed. My body started jerking around on the floor like I was having a seizure. As the last of the energy flowed into my body, it picked up the image of Superman and drove him through the top of my head and straight into my heart chakra, like another runaway locomotive.

Bam! Download number two.

The afternoons of the retreat were scheduled with classes. One of the teachers was a thirty-something gentleman from India, something like a modern-day guru. Because he was busy and lived far away, his lessons were provided via video. He spoke in a rather hypnotic cadence, and his eyes glazed over when he paused. It seemed as if he was plugged into an energy that most of us could only dream about. Carrying the qualities of peace and innocence, he was loved by everyone. It was impossible not to adore him.

On the last full day of the retreat, I wandered down to the beach for a stroll and some alone time. As I stepped from the path onto the beach, I distinctly heard someone call my name. I turned around and didn't see anyone, so I kept walking. After a few more steps, I heard my name again, this time loud and clear. Nobody was there! Remembering I was on a retreat and that no one around would really know me, I figured, *Okay. It's just my imagination.* But as I closed my eyes, I could see him plain as day, our modern-day Indian guru. By this time, I was starting to feel like I was losing my grip on reality.

Walking down the beach, we carried on a conversation that lasted about thirty minutes. He was very explicit and told me what I could expect over the next six months. It felt like being with a dear old friend. As we came to the end of the beach, he stood aside with an impish grin, as if he knew something. In a few seconds, we were joined by none other than Superman. Yes, this little rendezvous on the beach was happening in my imagination; however, the events were so lucid it was hard to distinguish between the imaginary and the physical world.

Seeing Superman walk toward me in such a no-nonsense, militaristic fashion sent a tingle of fear down my spine. He was there on business, and his business was with me. Off to the side, the guru was watching, trying not to laugh. Superman approached face-on, stopped about an arm's length away, and roared, "You just don't get it, do you?" As he said that, he smacked me on the chest with his open palm. I could physically feel the blow and was knocked back a step. The whole thing was becoming more bizarre by the moment.

Replying to his question, I imagined myself answering, "Uh...get what?" He responded, "Don't resist." I said, "Resist what?" With that answer, he wound up to hit me again. Instead of feeling his open palm slam into my chest, it passed right through into my torso. It felt extremely peculiar, even mind-boggling. I could feel him reaching inside my body, and he seemed to enjoy it. He kept pressing his hand from the surface to the inside of my body, as if he was testing something. With a growing smile, he said, "That's it! You're getting it!" On the next attempt to press into my chest, his entire arm entered my heart. At the same time, he did a kind of pirouette and completely entered my upper body, dissolving into my core. I looked over toward my guru friend for some kind of explanation, but he was gone. I was stupefied.

Download number three.

For three days after the retreat, I stayed in a hotel near a small port town. The previous week was incredibly intense. I was exhausted, in shock, and in need of rest. I had no idea what had happened, and it would take me months to piece it together. When I returned home, my life went on as usual. The only difference I noticed was that it felt as if my lower three chakras were blown wide open. I could feel it all the time.

About six months later, I returned to a follow-up retreat, given by the same organization. This time, it was in a different location, further from home. The routine was the same with classes and meditations, but the teachers weren't the same. They were all so young. Even though the information they presented was sound, it seemed as if they were simply parroting what they had learned in school. They lacked life experience, and I found it difficult to learn from teachers who had less experience and knowledge than I did. It wasn't arrogance on my part; something just wasn't ringing as true.

After five days, I was beginning to feel like I'd wasted my time and money. Nothing was happening: no insights, no mystical experiences, nothing. Nonetheless, there I was, so I had to try to make the best of it. It was a keep-the-ol'-chin-up sort of thing.

The last day of the retreat was my fiftieth birthday, and the final presentation was to be given that evening. To be quite honest, I was thinking about skipping it so I could go for an evening stroll. I really just wanted to go home. As soon as the group assembled, our instructor walked in. Much to everyone's pleasant surprise, it was our modern-day guru from the videos of the previous retreat. It was wonderful to see him there, flesh and blood.

Once again the surreal started to unfold. During the three-hour presentation, he frequently paused, as if connecting with the Divine, and stared into space with his eyes lightly glazed over. He consistently fixed his gaze in my direction, and I fell into a very deep trance. As our eyes connected, it felt as if waves of electricity were being transmitted from him to me. It was wild. This went on for about two hours. My remaining upper chakras were blown open.

Happy birthday! Download number four.

When I returned home, everything changed. My life completely imploded. Within a few weeks, I was living in a one-room basement apartment wondering, *What the hell just happened?* It was simple. I had gone through a complete internal transformation, and this marked the beginning of a new life. My inner life was being reflected out into my external world. Wherever I was going, I needed to let go of everything to get there, but it wasn't easy. In fact, it was devastating.

Even though I had worked with the subconscious mind for years, I was now emerging as a healer. The retreats opened me up to Divine energy; I could feel it come blasting through in my sessions. The healings that began to occur were phenomenal: cancer, depression, eating disorders, relationships, compulsive disorders, and anxiety attacks. It was uncanny.

However, I was going through my own process. My emotional state was a mess. Even though I was opened up to a much higher level of energy, I still had to do my own work. In fact, it was an integral part of the process. It made me a better healer because I had to heal myself. Fortunately, I wasn't all alone. I had a lot of help.

In the ensuing months, I thought about the retreats and wondered if my growth process was exclusively linked to that organization. Did they have the magic keys? After all, it sure worked for me. The idea of falling into a cult-like following was repelling, yet the experiences were so undeniable. Then something interesting happened.

As I was sitting in meditation one morning, I had the sensation that some gentle, yet strong male was placing his hands on my shoulders, transmitting energy into my heart. At the same time, I had the feeling some type of spiritual woman had her hands on my throat and forehead; her energy was gentle and warm. It went in deep, and I soaked it up like a sponge. This continued in my morning meditations for about two weeks. I suspected it was some kind of Divine download, but I wasn't sure. I needed evidence.

A couple days later, I went to the chiropractor. At the end of the session, he took out a tuning fork, gave it a whack, and slowly waved it over my entire body. I felt an immediate shift in my energy field, as if my aura had experienced a really good crack. That was my first exposure to sound healing, and I instantly recognized its enormous potential in subconscious healing. Two days later, a client brought in a set of tuning forks she never used and asked if she could trade them for a session. I've been using them ever since. There's your evidence.

I was especially grateful for the download that brought in the tuning forks. Not only did it add a new depth and dimension to my work, but I also no longer felt bound by the retreat organization. The Divine can come in any way it chooses. I was free.

Guardian Angels — Helpers and Friends

Guardian angels? I know people who swear by them as protectors of Divine will. I've heard numerous accounts and seen their helping hands in a number of difficult situations. I've even heard stories of angels slipping through the cracks of ether and visiting us in the physical world. However, those stories sounded like tall tales, some kind of wishful thinking. I was pretty skeptical until I went mountain climbing about twenty years ago.

In the early 1990s, I was living in a small mountain town. A friend and I decided to take a trip to the Olympic National Park in Washington State and climb Mt. Olympus. We had another friend in town who had just separated from his wife and kids. He was pretty down in the dumps, so we invited him along, figuring the trip could do him some good. His name was Trevor.

The first day of the trip consisted of an eighteen-mile hike from the trailhead to a shelter below tree line — an arduous hike for anybody, especially with climbing gear. Since we were all young and in pretty good shape, we figured we could handle it. We eventually dragged ourselves to base camp late in the day and went to bed early, knowing we had to be up at sunrise to hit the mountain.

After slogging all day and negotiating a little fog, we finally made it to the top. The last 100 feet consisted of a steep scramble that didn't require ropes. As we started up, Trevor decided to wait where he was; he didn't have the strength to make the rest of the climb. He had been a trooper all day and had not once complained, but we could tell his heart weighed about 10,000 pounds. His physical body was fine;

his strength was zapped by the burden he carried around his heart.

We made it back to the shelter by late afternoon and spent the rest of the day lying around, eating, and reading stories to each other. As the afternoon progressed, we heard something off in the distance and saw four people making their way up their trail. It was an East German family made up of a beautiful husband and wife with two skinny little girls, ages ten and twelve. They had emigrated from East Germany to Vancouver just before the Wall came down in 1988.

As we chitchatted away, I noticed some peculiarities. First, they didn't look particularly outdoorsy. In fact, they were very clean, with no dirt anywhere. According to them, they made the entire eighteen-mile hike that day, but it looked as if they hadn't even broken a sweat. I'm sorry, but there's no way they could have made that hike in one day with two skinny little kids. It was tough enough for us, three grown men with no little ones in tow!

Trevor began to talk to them in German. He wasn't fluent, but they humored him. They hadn't spoken much German in a while, and it reminded them of home. As the conversation continued, I noticed that the weight hanging over Trevor's heart started to lift. He cracked a smile, his eyes brightened up, and his face lifted. It was a good thing.

As they parted, we wondered where they were going to camp. It was only about 100 to 200 yards to the end of the trail, and there was nothing beyond that but boulders and snow. The rest of the surrounding area was heavily covered in brush, steep and strewn with rocks. They weren't going to be able to pitch a tent anywhere, let alone for four people. As we slowly came to that conclusion, we agreed we should invite them down to share our campsite, and Trevor took off to find them.

Fifteen minutes later, he came back, clearly perplexed. He couldn't find them, so we all went up to look for the family just to make sure nothing bad had happened. We looked everywhere, but there were no footprints and not even a campfire. They were nowhere to be found, and there was no place they could have gone. You can't hide a family in a tiny patch of woods, especially with two little kids. If they had come back down, they would have passed us. They wouldn't go ahead; hiking up the mountain at nightfall was nuts. They didn't seem crazy. They just…disappeared.

We shrugged our shoulders, went back to the shelter, got some sleep, and headed out the next morning. On the hike out, something amazing happened to Trevor. He was bursting with joy. The encounter he had with the family had generated deep spontaneous healing. He was full of optimistic hope, overflowing with elation, excited for all of life's possibilities. Either he was going through a complete personality change, or part of his personality was emerging after being repressed his entire life. It was a sight to see.

In the years since I have known Trevor, it has appeared that his personality shift was permanent. He's nowhere near the repressed guy he used to be. Ironically enough, he remarried and now has two skinny little stepdaughters of his own. He seems genuinely happy. To this day, he swears the family we met on the trail were his guardian angels.

Entities — Do You Believe in Ghosts?

Entities are disembodied beings that interact with the physical world. Some are naughty, and some are nice. They commonly get stuck on the Earth plane after a sudden or traumatic loss of life, as if death sneaked up on them so quickly and unexpectedly that they got disoriented. Most of them have lost their way and are looking for a path back home to the Divine. I've experienced entities more than a few times around hospitals.

I didn't believe in entities when I first started doing this work. Sure, I had heard stories, but I just brushed them off as the stuff of paranormal junkies hooked on woo-woo, just trash for late-night TV. However, experience has a way of changing things.

A few years back, I made an appointment to do a house call, and no, it wasn't to an abandoned castle on a cold, stormy night. Instead, it was log cabin in the woods on a beautiful spring day. I guided my client into a deep state of relaxation. As she floated away on a sailboat, I had the strange sensation of some kind of pressure pushing up against my face. The session went well, and I dismissed the pressure I felt as released subconscious compost. We scheduled another appointment for the next week, and I went home.

The following week, I returned and we resumed our work. About halfway through the session, as she entered a deep trance, I felt as if some nonphysical person was attacking me. My breathing was restricted, and I felt like I was being choked. My heart rate skyrocketed; I thought I was going to have a heart attack. Energetically, I was vehemently fighting to save my life. All the while, I was trying to conduct the healing session, as if nothing was wrong. I was horrified and had no idea what was happening. I eventually beat the thing back, whatever it was, ended the session, and went home. I couldn't wait to get out of there.

That afternoon, I met a friend of mine to go for a walk around a local lake. As we strolled, I became increasingly irritable and argumentative, which is not like me at all. I felt like I'd just slammed about sixteen cups of coffee. My heart was pounding so fast that I thought it would explode out my temples. I was sweating profusely. Something certainly was not right.

That night, after tossing and turning for about two hours, I finally drifted to sleep. I had a vivid dream where I released a baby alligator into a swamp. I immediately dove in after it. The gator had grown to full size and came after me with all it had, aiming to kill me. The ensuing battle seemed to last forever, but I eventually dispatched the beast and won a fight to the death. Had I lost that battle, I would have literally woken up dead.

The next morning, I rolled over and looked at the clock. It was noon! I couldn't believe it because I never sleep in like that. Furthermore, my sheets were soaked, and I was exhausted. It took all my strength to get out of bed. I sat on the edge of my bed and tried to figure out what was wrong. Then it hit me: "Oh God! I picked something up in the session yesterday!"

I immediately tried to contact my client, with no luck. After calling around, I eventually tracked down a relative, who told me she was in the hospital. My heart sank. She was admitted into emergency shortly after our session.

I took off for the hospital to see how she was faring. While I was driving, I had an intuitive flash that something was wrong with the right side of her torso. When I arrived at her room, she looked beat. She had contracted pneumonia in her right lung; it came on her immediately after our session. It was hard to believe because she had shown absolutely no signs of weakness the day before. Plus, she was triathlon athlete and was in tremendous shape. She wouldn't remember my visit.

Leaving the hospital, I was really scratching my head. What happened? As far as I could tell, there was an entity on her property, and it used the portal opened in the session as an escape route. Both of us were in the way and got mowed over. I bounced my theory off the professor of shamanic studies at the local university, and she concurred with my theory. Some angry entity had made an escape.

A few weeks later, my client had a few more healing sessions at her home with a polarity therapist. During each of the three sessions they had, a raven came to the back window and tapped on it. It was a bit eerie. After the third session, it flew off, never to return. My client fully recovered, and the entity was gone.

When the Divine Goes on Holiday — The Dark Night

So far, spiritual awakening has been fairly exciting, even outlandish at times. So to keep things from getting too routine or boring, the Divine takes a holiday. Just when you think you're getting the hang of spiritual interaction, all of a sudden...Poof! No Divine. It's the opposite of spiritual awakening. It probably has something to do with karmic balance or appreciating normal life as it is — or maybe it's just a reminder that the essence of Divine contact is rooted in mystery.

About a year ago, I was preparing to give a workshop. Ironically enough, the event centered on connecting to the Divine. A week or so before the workshop, I went into my daily meditation, the one where I sink into Divine connection and feel energy and tingling sensations throughout my body. On this particular day, I felt nothing. I was just sitting there watching my mind wander. I couldn't visualize or feel anything I considered to be of Divine connection. It had never happened before, and I was mildly alarmed. That week, my business also slowed considerably. I became a little depressed and felt very "normal" and lackluster. Actually, I think I felt naked. I've read about these experiences before, and they are often referred to as "the dark night of the soul."

With the workshop approaching and the Divine still absent, I began to dread the event. I was just going to have to fake it. I felt like a hypocrite of the worst kind, a spiritual hypocrite. However, the show must go on, so I bluffed my way through the workshop, teaching techniques and leading experiences I did not feel. It was very awkward.

When the workshop was over, I received a considerable amount of positive feedback. It was a huge relief. The Divine was still at work, even though I wasn't aware of it. Over the course of the next few weeks, my experience of the Divine drifted back into my life and my daily routine. My dark night of the soul wasn't that dark; it was just dim. To this day, I don't have any deep insights or revelations about what happened. The best I can come up with is that these things happen, and true joy lies in the appreciation of each new day.

Spiritual Skills and Techniques

Practice, Practice, Practice — The Divine Batting Cage

Growing up, I used to play a lot of baseball. I eventually got to the level of not too bad. In fact, the older I get, the better I used to be. Even though I loved to play, I found practice almost intolerably boring. Batting practice took forever and required a lot of standing around. It was the mechanics of the game without the excitement of competition. I guess it was like anything else: To get any good, you have to pay your dues.

So it is with spirituality, only without the boring parts. It's game day all the time. All you have to do is pay attention, which requires discipline and participation. Interaction with the Divine also takes motivation and initiative with a commitment to connect. Be it daily meditation, working in the garden, walking in Nature, listening to music, or driving down the highway; to deepen your relationship with the Divine, you must take the first step. The Divine will always respond. At that point, all you need to do is listen.

Continual Connection — Watering the Garden

Interaction with the Divine is a relationship. In a way, it's like any other. It's a give-and-take exchange that requires time and effort. Furthermore, as you grow and change, so will the relationship, because it's a mirror to your level of development. With water, the seeds you sow will grow.

Ideally, one day we'll all be ascended masters and saints with brilliant white halos drenched in Divine bliss. Sure, it's a nice idea, but how do you think that happens? It starts with practice and connecting every day, and that is followed by expansion. What's that? It's taking the experience in your daily practice and extending into your day-to-day life. It's developing a continual connection.

Let's say someone in their daily meditation experiences the Divine through feelings of peace combined with warm, tingly sensations in their heart. The next step is to be aware of those feelings when driving the car, at work, shopping, in interactions with others, and during other moments of the day. It's learning to gently focus and plug in all the time. It's repeatedly dissolving unawareness of Divine presence.

As continual connection improves, so will the quality of life. Stress decreases, problems vanish or become more manageable, synchronicity becomes commonplace, life flows, and you feel happy. Eventually, it will grow to the place where the Divine and you are one.

Feeling and Moving Energy — Playtime

Sooner or later, as you develop a relationship with the Divine, you'll begin to feel energy. Why? Because the Divine is energy, and that energy is filtered through us. It can be quite subtle. Furthermore, your experience with it won't be the same as anyone else's. However, many people feel sensations described as energy, electricity, or light, generally associated with some kind of movement. It might be in the body, outside of the body, or both. It will be unique to you, and it takes practice to develop the awareness.

When you begin to tune in to your energy field, you can start to play with it and move it around with intention or will. Again, this takes practice. As you become more accomplished at moving it around, you can begin to utilize it for specific tasks, such as healing or getting information. Take time to meditate to see if you can feel energy and then try and move it around.

In the early years of my first awakening, I began to become aware of energy that felt like small, slowly moving tornados, usually around my third chakra. I discovered I could pose certain questions to the energy, and if I could push the energy down toward my first chakra, the answer was "Yes." I saw the energy in my imagination and felt it in my physical body. What a discovery!

During this time, I was playing a lot of softball. I figured there was no better place to experiment than on the softball field. The first thing I noticed when I arrived at a game was that if I could push the energy down, we would win. Before every game, I could feel the outcome. I felt the shift when we rattled off seven wins in a row.

I also could take this newly developed skill onto the field, where I played shortstop. I was getting to the point where I could tell where the ball was going before it was hit. Prior to a pitch, I'd sneak this way or that way or come in a little. I was feeling the push and pull of the energy. I started getting the reputation of having pretty good range. But it wasn't that my range was all that spectacular; I just had a step or two of an advantage. It was like legal cheating! I loved it. (By the way, we did take first place that year.)

Manifesting — Future Progression

A friend of mine once told me, "There are two kinds of people in this world, those who say 'I can' and those who say 'I can't.' And ya know what? They're both right." The events in our lives are outward projections of what's lurking in our subconscious. That includes our thoughts, feelings, perceptions, and beliefs. We are who we think, feel, and believe we are. That goes for the good and the bad. If that's so, can we intentionally put thoughts, feelings, perceptions, and beliefs into the subconscious mind to create our future? The answer is: You bet! It's called manifesting.

Manifesting is simply utilizing the creative force of the subconscious by directing into the future. Anything is possible! The only limitation is what you can imagine. It's like applying a subconscious healing technique to the future. It can be applied to almost anything: healing, sports, technical skills, physical abilities, relationships, finances, health, etc. Roadblocks to manifesting show up as resistance and/or subconscious emotional charges. You'll need to use subconscious healing techniques from Lesson #4 to get rid of those.

Here's how it works: Get deeply relaxed and invoke the presence of the Divine. Next, imagine what it is you desire: an object, emotional state, lifestyle, relationship, finances, or anything else. See yourself with this desire and feel what would be like to possess it, as if you already have it. Allow the feeling of "having it already" to resonate deeply in your body and mind. Continue to feel and visualize your desire with absolute self-confidence, knowing that your desire will come. Feel "knowingness" deeply in your body, soak it in. Then let it go. To enhance the process, take action. Shop for a new car, start looking for your dream job, meet some people; do whatever you need to do to make it happen. Get involved in your process. Repeat all these steps until your desire appears.

If your desire doesn't arrive, watch out for any emotional charges that may come up and release them. If it still doesn't come, there may also be a timing component involved. Either way, stick with it.

Side Note: As your relationship with the Divine matures, manifesting won't be as important because you will be more centered in the present moment.

Intuition and Psychic Awareness

If I keep on this spiritual path will I be able to see the future? Will I need to get a crystal ball? Maybe. Learning to feel subtle energies, developing the ability to visualize, and releasing emotional charges will certainly sharpen your intuition. But what, exactly, is intuition?

Intuition is the direct perception of truth, independent of any reasoning process. It is information that doesn't come from the thinking mind. It might be an instinctual gut feeling (clairsentient), mental picture (clairvoyant), or auditory sound (clairauditory) that provides insight. Some people are extremely gifted at receiving and interpreting this kind of information, but it is also a talent that can be developed with practice and applied to any life situation.

Let's look at a fine example of intuition. A single friend of mine had a vision in his daily meditations that came to him over and over through the course of a year. It completely captured his attention because it was about his wife, a woman he had yet to meet. Every day he would sit, mesmerized by the clarity of the pictures. He knew the color of her hair, the shape of her eyes, and the depth of her personality. He even knew where she was from. He was so taken by these images that he became a bit obsessed. He thought he would meet her any day. After eight months went by and nothing happened, he decided to let it go, and the images faded.

Four years later at a business meeting, he met a woman and recognized her immediately. It was her, the woman from his meditations! He was somewhat in shock to find out she was single. Eventually, a relationship started up, and three years later, they were married.

Am I Making This Up? — Intuition vs. Manifesting

Sooner or later, you'll get to the point where you wonder if you're manifesting something or intuiting it. How can you tell when you cross the ambiguous gray area from intuition into manifestation? Where does creating end and destiny begin? Am I energetically creating something, or is it happening to me? What came first, the chicken or the egg?

I'm not sure. However, what I do know is that as you delve deeper into energetic pathways, you'll begin to think or feel a certain way about something, and it will happen. As resistance decreases and self-confidence increases, you'll step more into the creative flow of life. It's creating and being aware at the same time, like being the water in a moving river. Just make it up, and it will happen.

Spiritual Guides — We Are Not Alone

Are spirit guides real? I'm inclined to believe so, especially since I've seen their impact countless times in healing sessions. Let's say someone comes to see me for some nagging life issue. We may have some initial success, but nothing remarkable. As soon as we introduce a spirit guide into the picture, healing accelerates exponentially. There's an amazing comfort and influence in healing when you know you have help. It's tremendously reassuring to know we're not alone. Furthermore, they might actually be doing something.

Spirit guides can also impact personal growth, decision-making, and Divine downloads by providing insight, information, and energy. They show up in ways we can understand and assimilate, often awe inspiring or very peaceful states. The Divine likes to bring help in all ways that get our attention.

A while back, in my daily meditation, I was visited by a group of beings in human form. I was slightly surprised because I'm generally not a visual person. Although I'm not religious, I recognized the figures immediately as Moses, Jesus, Mary, Muhammad, Buddha, and Babaji. They formed a semicircle, and I referred to them simply as "the Council."

In the following two weeks, they visited every day. They never spoke a word but just sat, including me in their circle. However, what they did do was radiate an enormous amount of energy. I could feel it in my feet, hands, elbows, knees, and chest. It was an amazing experience, a Divine download.

When they finished, I could feel energy radiating out of me all the time, whenever I focused on it. It glowed especially strong out of my hands. I immediately began experimenting on willing clients to see if the energy could be transferred to facilitate healing. I used my hands and started hands-on healing. Over the course of a month, the feedback I received was consistently positive. Thanks to the Council, my healing ability took a quantum leap forward.

Divine Experience — Day-to-Day Applications

As you step more and more into your connection with the Divine, you'll begin to experience life as energy. The analogy that fits best for me is the flow of a river. It ebbs and flows with rapids, pools, and eddies. Although it can be slow, it rarely stops or grows stagnant. It's always moving, pushing along into growth. Sometimes it's effortless, while at other times it requires great exertion.

However, even during times of great exertion, there's always an underlying sensation of peace. As awareness develops, we learn to let go of resistance and actively ride in the flow. That requires surrendering to the Divine that we have learned to connect with. As we let go deeper into that surrender, we develop attributes of the Divine itself: peace, joy, and abundance, to name a few.

Following are a few random areas of life I've seen expressed as energetic flow within the Divine connection.

Money as Energy — Make Sure It's Clean

As you continue to experience and learn about the Divine and energy, you'll soon discover that money is a form of energy. It's an energetic flow of give and take. In the world of commerce, it's pretty obvious: You give me this, I pay you for that. There's an agreement. With inheritance, it's a little different.

For many people, inheriting money can be a strange and bittersweet experience. Why should I benefit because someone I love, hate, or don't care about dies? It can bring up a very mixed bag of emotions. Furthermore, with inheritance, there's no mutual agreement. It's pure one-way energy flow, an instant influx of power that may or may not be beneficial. When you inherit money from somebody, what you're really inheriting is their energy. It can either work wonders or bring misery. If the deceased's energy is not in alignment with the recipient, it can bring problems. Since money is energy, a sudden influx of it can blow up your energy field and all the subconscious emotional charges that live there. We have all heard stories of people who have won the lottery, and it destroyed their lives. The energy was too big, and their charges exploded.

I knew a woman whose mother was a tyrant and a very unscrupulous but successful businesswoman. They hadn't spoken for years. The mother accumulated a small empire based on dirty money. When she died, her daughter unwillingly hit the jackpot. Her financial concerns vanished because she received an inheritance from someone she hated. This unexpected windfall brought with it a stockpile of emotions, and she had a very difficult time coming to terms with the situation.

A while later, I met her for coffee, and it was obvious she had gone through a momentous personality change. She had starting drinking, and she was angry most of the time with a chip on her shoulder, just waiting for someone to knock it off. She had blown through an enormous wad of cash in short order. Her life was accelerating toward the bottom. I didn't know this person anymore; she had become her mother. It was if she was possessed by her mother's spirit.

A few years later, I saw her again. Her life was a wreck, but she had gotten on to the healing track. She was working through huge issues concerning her past and her mother, battling emotional and physical illness to the point of death. It was tough to witness her teetering on the brink, but I knew she was going to make it, and she did.

Relationships — You, Me, and Us

You are you, and I am me. We both have our own energy. That sounds simple enough, right? Right, but when you and I get together, a third energy shows up — and that's us. As the relationship develops, hopefully, we'll both maintain our own identity. However, the "us" in the relationship will also have its own personality and identity. It will be unique unto itself and different than any other us out there. It will also have its own purpose and destiny to fulfill, such as marriage, family, business, healing, sex, money, recreation, friendship, or teaching. Problems can arise when we try to force a relationship into something it's not destined to be. Examples may include pushing a friendship into marriage or going into business with a family member. Utilizing awareness, insight, and intuition can help us elude these potentially painful lessons.

Contracts as Energy — Bound by Agreement

As we go out in the world as little bundles of energy, so does everyone else. To get things done in life, we frequently merge our energies. In business and marriage, contracts are a common and formal way of merging energy. When two parties make an agreement and sign on the dotted line, their energies are bound indefinitely until the contract is mutually dissolved.

That said, if one member chooses not to honor the contract but takes no steps to dissolve it, their energy will still be bound. If the person has enough awareness, they'll actually be able to feel that drain of energy in their body. The entirety of their energy will not be available to them because it will be tied up in an agreement.

I've seen this situation played out in a number of marriages. Let's say a couple decides to split up but never gets around to actually filing for divorce and just lets it hang. As weeks, months, or years go by, their energies are still bound. There's a good possibility new relationships won't work out because the energy isn't available and is still tied to someone else. Plus, it's likely the grieving hasn't been completed. When they finally decide to divorce, repressed emotions of a failed relationship will likely surface, even if it's been years since the original split. Not until the divorce is complete will their energies be free.

Energy and Life Cycles — Don't Push the River

As you begin to discover life as the flow of energy, you may also start to notice the phenomenon of life cycles. Sure, there's the cyclical nature of the seasons: winter, spring, summer, and fall. These are the obvious rhythms of Nature. Similar to Nature, though, we have our own rhythms that can be as predictable and unstoppable as the seasons. The magic in life happens when we learn to flow with these cycles. A saying from Zen Buddhism refers to this wisdom: "Don't push the river."

Have you ever noticed that almost everyone goes through major life transitions around the ages of two, fourteen, twenty-one, thirty, forty-two, and fifty-six? Have you ever noticed that after a year of putting out major effort in your career, the next year is full of letting go and endings? Throughout the course of human history, these same questions have been pondered by ancient mystics. In their wisdom, they were able to develop systems of prediction to make sense of the human flow of life transitions. Two of the most prominent methods in the Western world are numerology and astrology.

I'm not an advocate of living your daily life based on these ancient systems; however, many times in life, I've seen these historic art forms make sense out of the seeming randomness of human existence. Studying the patterns of your personal life cycles can provide useful insight when negotiating the uneven terrain of life.

Life and Location — New York or LA?

Each of has our own energetic flavor that's unique to us. In slang, we call it a vibe. The same is true for places. Every country, state, region, city, and town has its own vibe. For example, let's say my personal vibration resonates to the color red, and New York vibes to yellow. If I live in New York, our colors will be combined to create the experience of orange. If LA resonates to blue, then when I move to LA, my experience will be purple.

What that means is that anyplace on this planet in which we choose to live will create unique life experiences for that place. There are certain themes for certain places, and this is tied into your personal astrology and associated with Earth energies.

When I lived in Boise, Idaho, my personal experiences were focused on authority, the law, career, day-to-day family life, and financial growth. There was little time or energy left for inward development. It wasn't the right place for me. When I moved to Bellingham, Washington, my life themes were focused on internal growth, spirituality, creativity, and healing. I made huge strides over short periods of time. However, themes centered on career and socializing just weren't going to fly there.

The same is true for all of us. Each of us experiences specific themes in specific locations, whether we're just visiting or residing there. For more insight into life themes and locations, search the Internet for "astro-cartography" and/or "relocation astrology."

Developing Sensitivity — Joy and Pain, the Two-Edged Sword

As your connection to the Divine expands and you become more aware of subtle life force energies, your sensitivity will increase. Your experience of life will deepen. That's wonderful and challenging, all in the same breath.

As your sensitivity develops, your emotional depth will expand enormously. Yes, there will be growing moments of joy and bliss beyond imagining. However, pain will run deep. Emotional charges will be felt with great acuity. You may be more sensitive to the suffering of the world at large. Environmental toxins, drugs, alcohol, and unhealthy foods may increasingly disturb your body. You may be required to give some things up.

On the other hand, your life will energize. As sensitivity increases, so will your connection to the Divine. You may develop healing ability, intuitive awareness, the desire to forgive, or compassion. Your ability to manifest and direct Divine energy will also become more acute. The person you are meant to be in this life will flower. Life will be forever transformed into something you never dreamt imaginable — a life filled with endless potential, opportunity, and excitement.

Lesson #5 — Homework

Congratulations! If you've made it this far, you deserve some time off! Keep up the good work, connect to the Divine daily, and enjoy life. No homework!

Lesson #6
Development Leads to Action

Mission (Not-So) Impossible

I've got Spiritual Skills — Now What?

Wow! I've connected to the Divine. I actually know what that means. I've even developed some spiritual skills. What's next? Now it's time to put it in gear, take it out in the world, and share it with others. Your life has improved, so go out and help others do the same.

The Ripple Effect of Healing

We are all beacons of radiating energy. Our subconscious is projected out into the world, for better or worse. If we take the time and energy to heal ourselves, healing will expand all around us. Miracles will start to happen. Seemingly without any effort on our part, people around us will benefit. Not only will the quality of our own lives improve, but also the lives of everyone we come in contact with. It turns into a positive cycle of regeneration, healing others by doing nothing but healing ourselves.

I had a friend who was a child of alcoholic parents. After his mom died, his dad lost it and went completely off the deep end. The only way he knew to deal with his grief was to crawl into his bottle. His behavior grew very bizarre, and his physical health began to deteriorate. He was dying, killing himself with grief and alcohol, and it wasn't going to take long.

My friend's family had fragmented over the years due to all the drinking. Everyone had drifted apart, and it appeared, contentedly so. When his dad crashed, he and his siblings rallied for one last effort to pull the troops together in the form of an intervention.

Even through the delirium of alcohol abuse, his father was a dedicated family man. His children and grandchildren meant everything to him, so when they dropped the ultimatum, "Quit drinking or you'll never see us again," he entered a clinic that day. He spent three long weeks at an inpatient rehab facility.

The healing he went through was nothing short of miraculous. He was able to sift through his grief and process an assortment of issues related to his past, and he never touched a drop of alcohol again. As he continued on his path of recovery, the entire family started to reconnect. The relationships continued, even after his dad died. The father's love and courage, required to face his own healing, was the glue that brought the family back together.

The Greatest Service — Be Yourself

I remember something my second grade teacher always told us: "Be yourself." I wasn't quite sure what she meant. The funny thing was, at forty, I still didn't know. Life is a gift from the Divine. The greatest achievement we can attain in this life is to be the fullest expression of who we really are.

Sounds simple, but is it? When we come into this world, we enter as a blank slate, but each of us has a specific destiny to fulfill. It may be related to something the world values, like a career, but we must realize the values of society can be skewed. Maybe our destiny is something society doesn't monetarily recognize, value, or understand. Perhaps it's about inward development, raising a family, learning about compassion, or balancing the scale for past karmic debts. It can take a lifetime to find out who we genuinely are.

The journey toward self-discovery begins in the releasing of subconscious emotional charges. Why? Because emotional charges are obstacles to Divine connection. Clearing those barriers allows us to begin the journey into the mysteries of that Divine union. When that happens, who we are will effortlessly emerge.

Passion, Purpose, Meaning, and Mission — Go Get 'em, Tiger!

Nothing stokes the fire of Divine action like passion, meaning, mission, and purpose. Adding these spices to the palette of life will add spark to Divine fulfillment.

Passion
Passion is the road sign to self-discovery, a flashing beacon pointing out the quickest and most direct route to the Divine. The desires of your heart are imprinted with Divine thumbprints. Whatever gets you excited, consumes your attention, and brings joy when you wake up in the morning is nothing short of a Divine occupation. It's where your

truest sense of yourself will be found. Passion is a call to your homeland.

Meaning

A few weeks ago, I was walking along a major construction site in town. An old private paper mill had been torn down. Through extensive negotiations, the land had been turned over to the public for redevelopment, to include shops, parks, a marina, and open space.

A crew of bricklayers working there were on their break, and I asked them what they were working on. One guy said, "Oh, just laying some brick. Pays the bills, ya know?" The chap standing next to him said, "Actually, this is a pretty cool project. It's the entry to the new waterfront." A third worker smiled and chimed in, "I'm building the future."

The meaning of life is straightforward; life holds whatever meaning you give it. If you feel your life has no meaning, it's only because you haven't given it any. Don't forget that we are co-creators of Divine will. We can make our lives as big or small as we choose, based on our perception. Remember George Bailey from *It's a Wonderful Life?* His life presumably had no meaning...until he shifted his perception. The reason my life has meaning is because I say it does. If you want a meaningful life, then believe it and go live it that way.

Mission

One way to live a meaningful life is to have a mission. What's a mission? It's an important task given to you straight from the Divine. If you want meaning in life then get on with your mission. It may take anywhere from one day to a lifetime. That's up to you. Who decides what it is? You do! A mission takes the concept of a co-creative relationship with the Divine and puts it into action. In terms of livelihood or vocation, think of it this way: Do you have a job, a career, or a mission?

Purpose
Several years ago, I went to a three-part workshop that met on Wednesday nights. On the first evening, the facilitator posed the question: "Would you like to know the purpose of life? It's really simple." Intrigued with anticipation, we all nodded with inquisitive approval. "Good," she said. "I'll tell you next week." Ha-ha. Very funny. The following week, she posed the same question. This time, everyone rolled their eyes with suspicion. Disappointed, she answered, "Hmmm...Looks like you're not ready. I'll tell you next week." Now she had our attention. In our last meeting, she didn't mention the question at all. As we were packing up to leave, one of the participants asked, "Well? Are you going to tell us the answer? What is the purpose of life?" With a slight smirk on her face, she replied, "The purpose of life is living...so get on with it."

Helping Others

As your spiritual life unfolds into a deeper connection with the Divine, you'll be busy in the art of living, experiencing life to the fullest. Joy and peace will be natural byproducts. Joy will create more joy, and peace will create more peace. It won't be possible to keep it to yourself. You'll want to share the Divine connection with others.

Maybe you'll be drawn into specific types of service, like healing or alleviating the suffering of others in some way. Perhaps your joy will spill over to the nurturing of the planet. Maybe it will be sharing abundance or teaching others how to connect into the Divine. Whatever it is, your natural inclination to help others will blossom from your passion of living.

Homework

Get yourself situated in a nice meditative position. Drift into a deeply relaxed state. While you're there, invoke the presence of the Divine and ask for help. Feel it deeply, knowing that what you ask is on the way. Call up feelings of passion, meaning, mission, and purpose, and allow those feelings to direct your attention to action that will fulfill those attributes. Then go do it!

Appendix

Summary

1. Pain Leads to Suffering

We all feel pain. Because pain is uncomfortable, we have a tendency to unknowingly repress unpleasant emotion into our subconscious. These painful feelings are called subconscious emotional charges. You can feel them in your body, and the repeating patterns of pain they create are known as suffering.

2. Suffering Leads to Awareness

Recognizing subconscious emotional charges and where they are felt in the body are the first steps in healing. It's also a necessary step toward spiritual growth. When we have suffered enough, we begin to look for the sources of our suffering. These can come from a variety of experiences, but they all originate in the past. Some universal themes of suffering include abandonment, unworthiness, grief, physical illness, resistance, stress, and addictions.

3. Awareness Leads to Healing

Once we become aware of subconscious emotional charges and painful repeating patterns, we can take active steps to heal the subconscious. There are numerous techniques to accomplish this, but each technique is essentially a form of meditation that will enable us to feel repressed emotion and let it go.

4. Healing Leads to Awakening

The subconscious mind is the home of subconscious emotional charges. It's also the path to the Divine. As subconscious healing advances, connecting with Divine energy will happen naturally, through our energy field and chakras. We can develop this connection by utilizing the vastness of the imagination. This can be achieved through deep states of relaxation.

5. Awakening Leads to Development

As connection to the Divine is established, mystical experiences may begin to occur. Spiritual skills can also be developed, which may include creating constant interaction with Divine energy, sharpening intuition, moving energy, manifesting, and healing.

6. Development Leads to Action

As your connection with the Divine unfolds, you'll discover the highest expression of yourself in connection with that energy. Your life will fill with passion, meaning, purpose, and joy. You won't be able to prevent yourself from taking action; you'll want to share it with others. For some, the act of just being themselves is enough.

References

Arjuna, Ardagh, *Awakening into Oneness: The Power of Blessing in the Evolution of Consciousness.* (Louisville, Colorado: Sounds True, Inc., 2007) p. 211.

Eastman, David T., Kundalini Demystified, *Yoga Journal* (September 1985): pp. 37–43.

Edie, Bev, Chakra map, Original artwork. Bellingham, WA, 2011.

Havens, Ronald A. and Catherine Walters, *Hypnotherapy Scripts,* 2nd Edition (East Sussex, United Kingdom: Brunner-Routledge, 2002) p. 280.

It's a Wonderful Life. Director Frank Capra. Performers James Stewart, Donna Reed, Lionel Barrymore, and Henry Travers. Liberty Films/RKO Pictures, 1946.

Javane, Faith and Dusty Bunker, *Numerology and the Divine Triangle* (West Chester, Pennsylvania: Whitford Press, 1979) p. 265.

Jenny, Hans, *Cymatics: A Study of Wave Phenomena & Vibration,* 3rd Edition (New Hampshire: MACROmedia Publishing, 2001) p. 295.

Judith, Anodea, History of the Chakra System, Last modified
    October 28, 2004,
    http://www.yoga.com/ydc/enlighten/enlighten_docume
    nt.asp?ID=341&section=9&cat=.

Nelson, Bradley, *The Emotion Code,* 2007, Wellness
    Unmasked Publishing, p. 383.

Oswald, Yvonne, *Every Word Has Power* (Hillsboro, Oregon:
    Atria/Beyond Words, 2008) p. 208.

Parkhill, Stephen, *Answer Cancer* (Deland, Florida: Omni
    Hypnosis, 1995) p. 219.

Tolle, Eckhart, *A New Earth: Awakening to Your Life's Purpose*
    (New York: Penguin/Dutton, 2005) p. 336.

Additional Resources and Information

Joseph D. Drumheller, Healing Arts Professional:
    www.josephdrumheller.com

Byron Katie: www.thework.com

EFT (Emotional Freedom Techniques):
    www.eftuniverse.com

The Body Talk Center: www.thebodytalkcenter.com

Oneness University: www.onenessuniversity.org

About the Author

Joseph D. Drumheller has been practicing the art of healing since 1991. From 2003-11, he worked extensively with cancer patients at the PeaceHealth Cancer Center in Bellingham, WA. His mission lies in helping people overcome all forms of suffering and to learn how to connect to Divine presence. His own relationship to the Divine is expressed as a deep love for the outdoors, which he pursues as an avid whitewater paddler, boat-builder, visual artist, writer, musician, and geologist. He lives in Spokane, Washington with his twin flame Tamara.

My value is equal to everyone else

Printed in the USA
CPSIA information can be obtained
at www.ICGtesting.com
LVHW010431241223
767241LV00007B/726